Conservation of a rare animal is an issue which justifiably looms large in this age of population explosion and continuous industrial growth. Bruce Wright combines in this book his scientific interest in conservation and his sensitivity for the wilderness and its inhabitants in his presentation of a case for the little-known eastern panther. This animal has long been thought extinct by many, and has therefore remained unprotected by the passage of laws. In an effort to secure such legal security for this sub-species of the panther, Bruce Wright has gathered impressive evidence that this animal has indeed managed to survive in small numbers in eastern Canada and the United States.

During his years as Director of the Northeastern Wildlife Station in New Brunswick, the author has accumulated hundreds of reports from individuals who have actually seen an eastern panther. From New Brunswick and Nova Scotia, Quebec and Maine, Vermont, New Hampshire and other states of the eastern United States letters have come, describing when and where sightings have occurred. Many of these have been reproduced in the text, and describe not only interesting habits of the animal itself, but also tell a great deal about the way of life in rural eastern Canada and the United States.

Other chapters in the book discuss the physical traits and habits of the eastern panther, and the methods of field study which conservationists use regarding it. But the main emphasis throughout is on the presentation of evidence for the existence of the animal, and the plea that it be protected by law as a rare species.

# THE EASTERN PANTHER

# The Eastern Panther

*A Question of Survival*

Born in Quebec City, *Bruce S. Wright* was an excellent athlete and marksman in his school and college days. His degree in Forestry led him to a post with the Dominion Forest Service. He served with the Canadian Navy during the war. (A previous book, *The Frogmen of Burma*, relates his part in the formation and commanding of the Sea Reconnaissance Unit.)

Subsequently he carried out graduate study in Wildlife Management and has become Director of the Northeastern Wildlife Station at the University of New Brunswick. His career as a writer began in 1938 with articles on conservation, and he has continued to write articles and books on wildlife. In addition to *The Frogmen of Burma*, he is the author of *Black Duck Spring* and other works.

by Bruce S. Wright

*with drawings by Robert Hines*

CLARKE, IRWIN & COMPANY LIMITED   TORONTO / VANCOUVER / 1972

Drawings by Robert Hines courtesy of the
Frederic C. Walcott Memorial Fund of the
North American Wildlife Foundation

# *Foreword*

The big cats that roam the north woods and the mountainous regions of eastern North America stir the imagination of outdoor lovers as no other group of animals. The bobcat, the lynx and the panther are synonymous with the eerie shadows of evening along a wilderness tote road. The panther is the largest, rarest and most secretive of the cats, and has been the subject of folk tales and hair-raising stories ever since the white man began hewing a living out of the New World wilderness.

The eastern panther is known by various other names, including cougar, mountain lion, catamount, Indian Devil. By whatever name it has been called in the northeastern United States and eastern Canada, it has seldom been seen, even in the early days. Tales of such sightings always aroused in the listeners a mixture of emotions—fear, awe, spine-tingling chills; but also admiration for the cunning and skill of the glamorous great beast of the big woods. Its numbers have gradually dwindled, and soon after the turn of the century the eastern panther was believed to be extinct save for a remnant population in the remote swamps of the deep south.

Yet, occasional mountain lion reports continued to filter in from Quebec to Pennsylvania and east to the Bay of Fundy. Most of these were ridiculed and put down to either a combination of vivid imagination and dim light, or else to the result of too much firewater.

By the mid-1940's, most biologists had accepted the view that the panther no longer existed in the northeast. About that time Bruce Wright became Director of the Northeastern Wildlife Station in Fredericton, New Brunswick. He gradually became impressed by an increasing number of cougar reports in that province and in surrounding regions. He began investigating and cataloguing the sightings. As evidence increased, both in volume and in quality—even though circumstantial—Mr. Wright became convinced that small local populations still existed. Eventually, track casts were identified as panther by internationally-known authorities. Sightings by reputable people became more numerous. Two specimens from the northeast, although not freshly examined by professional biologists, appeared quite definitely to have been taken during the 1930's.

For more than twenty years Bruce Wright and his staff members have painstakingly catalogued all details of every panther report available. On-the-spot investigations and personal interviews were made where possible. This book is the result of the long study. The evidence is arranged chronologically as well as geographically. It permits the reader to draw his own conclusions from case histories, both weak and strong. Most readers will probably agree with Mr. Wright that a small population of panthers still exists in portions of the eastern United States and Canada. They will also agree with him that the animals should not be persecuted.

Bruce Wright has written this volume partly for the biologist—to bring together under one cover all existing information on the eastern race of one of the continent's most interesting animals. But more than that, he has written for those whose everyday lives or hobbies take them into the outdoors—the woodcutter, trapper, hunter, fisherman, and the householder, living in the isolated, unpainted farmhouse bordering the northern woodland. As he states in the introduction, his objective is to relate the panther story "in a manner that will entertain as it educates." This he does. Moreover, entirely apart from its main subject, this book gives us frequent and vivid accounts of the rural people of New Brunswick and their land.

There are probably a few biologists who will still question that the existence of the panther in the northeast has been proven—lacking a *freshly killed* specimen, long a scientific criterion of distribution records. But much of Mr. Wright's evidence will satisfy all but the most critical. Certainly, the New Brunswick and Quebec data cannot be doubted. Evidence from adjacent areas is not as voluminous and not quite as convincing, but it nevertheless provides a strong case for scattered, local populations of panthers. As for my own State of Maine, I believe, from the data presented, that we probably have a few "Injun Devils" left. I hope that we do, for otherwise some of the mystery, fascination and nostalgia of the north country would be gone.

HOWARD L. MENDALL

*Office of the Leader*
*Maine Cooperative Wildlife Research Unit*
*October 1971*

# Introduction and acknowledgements

Of all the animals of North America, the panther of the north-east must lead one of the most lonely lives. Widely spread over great distances, it must have developed the ability to survive in incredibly small numbers. This presupposes a high degree of mobility and a low mortality rate. Small wonder then, that with no hunting, years go by between deaths of individuals, and many more years between deaths of individuals that fall into the hands of man.

Between these rare and widely spaced instances when a panther falls into the hands of man, its only contact with him is a fleeting glimpse of an almost unknown animal appearing for a few seconds with no warning crossing a road. Yet they are seen by men far more frequently than is commonly supposed. Not until someone with the necessary skills, knowledge, opportunity, and persistence comes along and makes a collection of these appearances over a period of years does it become apparent that these shy, usually silent, and solitary creatures are seen by man every year over a vast area.

I have made such a collection, both of historical references dating back to the earliest records, and live reports dating from the early 1940's. This book is a condensation of these records into the story of the survival of the species until today.

Recently I wrote one of our leading scientists who had just written a book on the mammals of eastern Canada and asked him why he had ignored the Little St. John Lake specimen of the eastern panther, the account and photograph of which was published in the *Journal of Mammalogy* (42, (2), May 1961). He replied because it was not seen *in the flesh* by a scientist.

The number of eastern panthers that scientists have examined *in the flesh* must be very small. Usually only the skin and skull, and occasionally the skeleton, has reached the scientist, and they are in the museums today. I very much doubt if any of the Canadian specimens could meet this test.

In this book I have cast a much wider net. I believe that pulp-cutters and farmers, game wardens and Royal Canadian Mounted Police officers, judges and doctors, foresters and veterinary pathologists, a Director of a Provincial Parks system, a Master of

Science in Wildlife Management who is the director of a wildlife research station, and two Ph.D. zoologists all have something to tell us. They have not only seen this animal in the flesh, *but they have seen it alive in the wild.* Their evidence seems worth recording.

In order to do this it has been necessary to take the evidence where it can be found. This includes sources that are normally unacceptable in scientific investigations, such as newspaper accounts. All such accounts in this book have been verified as far as it is possible to do so. However, in the older accounts the principals are dead and it is necessary to accept the story as it stands, or reject it entirely. I have made this decision based on the now-known history of the animal in the area, and I take full responsibility for their inclusion here. In my judgement they belong.

The objectives of this book are threefold. Firstly, to examine the most important evidence for the animal's continued existence. Secondly, to outline a course of action to ensure that it continues to exist. The third objective is to tell the story of one of the rarest and least known of all the native animals of North America in a manner that will entertain as it educates. We have reached the stage today when we can set aside several thousand square miles as an inviolate sanctuary for about fifty cranes to nest in, and we can successfully oppose the United States Air Force to protect their winter home. We can burn a forest in Michigan to provide proper nesting conditions for about a thousand rare warblers weighing in total about thirty pounds, and few object. The strides forward in conservational thinking and action are fantastic since I first began the long and often thankless task of collecting panther records in the northeast.

Perhaps the time has come at last to consider what protection, if any, the panthers need. Is the oft-repeated cliché, "If no more are killed in the next fifty years than were killed in the last, they need no protection" good enough? Or is this the "Locking the door after the horse is stolen" philosophy? Will the sight of one still arouse the same primitive instincts it did in the two Caddo County, Louisiana deputies when on November 30, 1965 they saw a panther on the road.

"They chased him into the wooded areas, first wounding him with a .357 Magnum, which only paralysed him. They finished him off with a shot gun." (*Shreveport Times,* December 1, 1965).

This was the first panther seen in the state in forty years. Fortunately its dead body reached the museum of Louisiana State University where it will be of permanent value, but was it really necessary to kill it? Was it doing any harm? Or was it simply trying to cross the road unseen? No one asked or answered these questions, but Wayne Chastain of the *Times* wrote: "A seven-foot panther—shot near Keithville and placed in deep freeze here yesterday—may be Louisiana's last link with a pioneer and primitive past."

Is this good enough today? Surely these lonely survivors should be granted the status of at least a game animal protected by closed seasons, if it is too much to ask that a large predator, although at a dangerously low level for many years, be given complete protection. Bounties have at long last been removed in every state and province of North America except South Dakota and Texas. Sport hunting has been substituted in those parts of the west where the local mountain lion population will stand it. In the midwest and the east there are no such populations left. The Florida panther, and the remaining animals in southern Alabama and Georgia, have been placed under the protection of the Office of Endangered Species of the U.S. Fish and Wildlife Service, and New Hampshire has set the precedent in the northeast and declared the species a protected animal. But how long will it be before such protection is extended everywhere east of the Mississippi and into central and eastern Canada?

When it is, the panthers will not even know it, for in order to survive until today they have automatically avoided man with all the wonderful skills at their command. They will not change.

This book has been written with a greater degree of enthusiasm and in a different style than most non-fiction books. It is hoped that this enthusiasm will become contagious and even recruit a friend or two for the solitary ones back on the hills. They are going to need all the friends they can get.

The first person to take an active interest in my study of the survival of the panther in the northeast was the late Dr. R. M. Anderson of the National Museum of Canada. He was followed by the late Professor Aldo Leopold of the University of Wisconsin. Dr. Ira N. Gabrielson of the Wildlife Management Institute of Washington was next, and finally there was Stanley P. Young of the United States Fish and Wildlife Service, who identified the track casts.

The Wildlife Management Institute of Washington provided financial support. The publication of this book was supported by a grant from the Northeastern Wildlife Station at the University of New Brunswick. The art work was supported by a grant from the Frederic C. Walcott Memorial Fund of the North American Wildlife Foundation.

In New Brunswick I am indebted to Dr. C. W. Argue, retired Dean of Science at the University of New Brunswick, for encouragement and advice over a twenty-year period. Freeman McKnight of Sussex was one of the earliest cooperators in the field.

In Nova Scotia, Robie W. Tufts, then the Federal Migratory Bird Officer for the Maritime Provinces; Dr. Harrison F. Lewis, retired chief of the Canadian Wildlife Service; Lloyd Duncanson, Taxidermist, the Nova Scotia Museum; Denis Benson, then Wildlife Biologist of the Department of Lands and Forests; Dr. Donald Dodds of Acadia University; and Ashford Fox of Amherst all contributed to the study.

In Quebec, Wildlife Technician Jacques Normandin led me to the Little St. John Lake specimen, and Dr. C. H. D. Clarke contributed Ontario reports.

In the United States, Ludwig K. Moorehead of New York City, and the late Herbert Ravenel Sass of Charleston contributed many reports. In Maine, Howard L. Mendall, Gene Letourneau, Henry Plummer and White Nichols all made important contributions. In New Hampshire, Mrs. Helenette Silver and Charles Larned Robinson contributed material.

To all of these my thanks are expressed.

BRUCE S.WRIGHT

*Fredericton, New Brunswick*
*October 1971*

# Contents

Foreword / v
Introduction and acknowledgments / vii
Prologue / 1

one
In the beginning / 3

two
The panthers of eastern Canada / 15
    New Brunswick
        Southwest Range / 15
        Western Range / 22
        Base Gagetown Range / 32
        Central Range / 36
        Juniper Range / 50
        Northwest Range / 56
        Restigouche-Nepisiguit Range / 57
        Miramichi Range / 62
        Kent-Westmorland Range / 68
        Southern Range / 70
    Nova Scotia / 79
    Quebec / 88
    Ontario / 95

three
Recent reports from the eastern United States / 97

four
The animal / 113

five
Methods of field study / 129

six
Some sighting sequences and their interpretations / 139

seven
The future—status and research needs / 145

appendix I
Selected panther reports from eastern Canada / 155

appendix II
Selected panther reports from the eastern United States / 164

Panther observations used in this book / 166
Bibliography / 167
Index / 178

The panther ranges of New Brunswick.
(Northeastern Wildlife Station.)

# *Prologue*

As this book is being written, a huge cat, but not of the four-legged kind, is smashing through the dense forest of the Fundy Hills. It is bulldozing out new hauling roads and it is followed by the whine of power saws and the roar and clatter of trucks as they haul away the pulp in billowing clouds of dust. This dust is the very thin topsoil of these ancient hills. Seas of slash, stumps and churned-up boulders mark the remorseless advance of the woods operation, already five miles into the wilderness area.

At a lodge not far away a meeting was held recently to promote yet another scheme to complete the ruin of the roadless wilderness between St. Martins and the Fundy National Park. The subject of this meeting was the promotion of the proposed Fundy Trail, a new highway to follow the shores of the Bay of Fundy and increase public access, with all the attendant ruin of natural areas that goes with it.

This country is a breeding area of the eastern panther, an animal long thought to be extinct and one that is still exceedingly rare. It is, in fact, the *only* known breeding area with definable boundaries. Eastern panthers have bred there for at least fifty years and are there today. (An immature specimen was seen in the Fundy National Park just east of the area on June 13, 1971.) They may be able to survive the disturbance of the pulpwood operation, if enough of the original forest remains, and in the long term it may improve their range as the deer move into the new growth.

However, if on top of this great upheaval in their solitude-loving lives is added the long-term disturbance occasioned by the construction of a major highway through the heart of the area, followed by the permanent opening up of the region, the end of the Martin Head Panther Range is in sight.

The ironic aspect of the situation is that in such a case the eastern panther would be wiped out before it legally existed. The animal is still not officially recognized, except in New Hampshire and Florida, and without such recognition protection by law is not possible. Legal safeguards are desperately needed to protect this rare creature and to prevent it from vanishing from the earth.

# Chapter 1
## In the beginning

When I first told my then teacher and good friend, the late Aldo Leopold, that there were still panthers in the forests of New Brunswick he was as incredulous as everyone else. Later, after we had examined the evidence, his first words were: "We must not tell anybody." This reaction was typical of perhaps the deepest thinker the wildlife field has yet produced.

His first thought was to preserve this surviving remnant of a subspecies long thought to be extinct, and his fear was of the kind of "sportsman" with unlimited means who will do anything to get the last, or the biggest, or the finest of any rare species. Such there are, and a rare panther would be irresistible to them.

This problem of keeping quiet, and at the same time asking the Game Department to help, was to cause me much trouble, as for some time my actions were regarded with deep suspicion by certain officials. However, the curtain could not be drawn for long as the newspapers already carried accounts of panther sightings, and it soon became apparent that the time had come "to get our licks in first." The August 1948 issue of the *Journal of Mammalogy* carried my paper "Survival of the Northeastern Panther (*Felis concolor*) in New Brunswick," and it was followed by the article "The Fundy Lions" in the September issue of *Field and Stream*. The cat was out of the bag.

The response was about as expected: scepticism in most quarters from those who had not considered the evidence, but none from those who had. We were prepared for this, and we had achieved our objective. We had established in the eyes of the public and the press that here was a subject in which we were vitally interested and would respond at once if asked for information. This insured that we would receive reports promptly.

Still, it was a two-edged sword, as the story made fascinating reading and thus drew attention to the very animals we were hoping to shield from the wrong kind of publicity. But right from the beginning the point was made that these were very rare and shy creatures that were doing no harm and should not be molested. We hammered this home at every opportunity.

The Game Department was not helpful. Their thinking at that time was in the order of "bring me the dead body and nothing else and I will believe you. Not before." Casts and photographs of tracks, identified by the highest authorities, were simply ignored. Deer kills were shrugged off as the work of bobcats, dogs, or bears, and eyewitnesses were just not believed. It was very simple, and no one had to take any action and everyone was happy—except the frustrated eyewitness who went away muttering "I wasn't drunk—and I did see it!" In time the eyewitnesses learned to come to the Wildlife Station, where their stories were taken seriously. This book tells you what they told us, and what we did with the information.

The centre of New Brunswick is still today a great forest of over 20,000 square miles in area. This forest is broken by roads and settlements along some of the main watercourses, but you only have to fly over it to see how small the "holes in the woods" man has made really are, compared to the total area. This forest probably was the area of survival of the breeding nuclei of panthers that have extended their range into eastern Maine, Quebec and Nova Scotia.

A panther report requires a man and a panther. Where one or the other is missing there are no records. There are relatively few men in the centre of the great New Brunswick forest, and for this reason most reports come from the forest edge behind the settlements. Some areas can be considered as separate ranges as they are divided from the main forest by major settlements. These lie in the southwest corner between the settled St. John Valley and Maine. It should be remembered that the international boundary means nothing in discussing ranges of wild animals and is merely a convenient stopping place at which to terminate a study.

At the close of the Pleistocene Period the land mammals of North America reached their peak in size. The grass-eaters were preyed upon by the greatest predators this continent has ever known: the sabre-toothed tiger, the California lion, and the giant dire wolf. The great herds of horse-like and camel-like animals roaming the grasslands, and the primitive forerunners of the deer in the forests provided their food. Toward the end of this period, when the great predators were beginning to disappear, a much less formidable cat was evolving which was smaller and more secretive in its habits. It contented itself with the smaller animals from the size of deer down, and it was most successful.

Gradually the land mammals changed from the horse-like and camel-like creatures to the forefathers of the buffalo, the pronghorn, and the deer as we know them today. As these extremely slow changes took place the great predators who had no enemies, and consequently no fear, began to die out. The Recent Period had arrived. The panther was a relative newcomer to the fauna of central and eastern Canada. It only appeared after the final recession of the Wisconsin Glacier about 8,000 years ago. It replaced the sabre-toothed *Smilodon*, a short-tailed cat, as the largest of the *Felidae*. At this time the Mastodon, the dire wolf, and the giant deer with their ten-foot antlers, were disappearing, and their modern counterparts were taking over.

The huge dire wolf of the Pleistocene was succeeded by the grey buffalo wolf of the plains, and the secretive smaller cat emerged as the most successful of this very versatile family. Thus came upon the scene of our continent the animal we know today as the panther, mountain lion or cougar, among other names. So successful was it, and so admirably did it adjust to the virgin lands of North America, that it soon covered the continent from Atlantic to Pacific, and as far north as the deer ranged.

This range took panthers into southern Canada where they learned to winter in heavy snow in the east and central parts, along the high mountains in pursuit of mule deer in the west (where they reached their farthest north), and into the heavy timber and coastal islands of the Pacific Coast after the diminutive blacktails. To the south they thrived in the central Rocky Mountain region, and followed the cover of the river valleys out onto the grasslands where they preyed on plains game as it came to drink. In the eastern mountains they were once again back in familiar deer country, and they followed these animals south to the flatlands of Florida until the mangrove jungles ringing Florida Bay ended their wanderings in that direction.

In the arid southwest they roamed from desolate sun-baked

mountain ranges, to the cactus flats, and along the rivers at the bottom of great canyons where they varied their diet with occasional small mammals. Versatile and adaptable to the extreme, nothing but unbroken stretches of true desert stopped them in their wanderings. Crossing northern Mexico they left the arid country for the tropics, and became jungle animals, hunting monkeys, agoutis, and the larger tapir, in addition to the inevitable deer. Across the land bridge to South America they spread, but in this Central and South American region they met for the first time a member of their own family that was their superior in size, strength and ferocity.

In northern Mexico they first noticed great pug marks at the waterholes that were larger and heavier than their own. At night they heard the coughing roar of the male jaguar, and they prudently withdrew from his territory. For the first and only time there was a rival they must respect. Here they were no longer the unquestioned lords of all they surveyed.

Down the mighty spine of the Andes they lived in much the same manner as they had in the Rockies, but added to their diet llamas, vicuñas, guanacos, and several new kinds of deer and rodents. As the savannahs of the Mato Grosso merged into the open pampas to the south they were back again in the living conditions of the American prairies, but now the three-toed ostrich-like rheas replaced the pronghorns of North America. They did not stop until they had reached the southern extremity of the mainland at the Strait of Magellan, and here the great silver-grey pumas that are thought to be the largest of their kind added the final touch to the vast scope of their diet. On these lonely and desolate beaches the lithe grey cats stalked the young of the mighty sea lions hauled up on the rocks, and carried them off to caves in the cliffs to devour.

Thus from the Yukon border in 60° north latitude in Canada to the Strait of Magellan in 53° south latitude in Patagonia did the lesser cat that emerged from the Pleistocene establish its vast range. No other land mammal was so successful.

This was the situation when the first men appeared in North America across the land bridge from Asia. This newcomer was inspected by the great cat as a possible addition to its diet, but a few trials showed that men were inferior to deer and the other natural foods available. The attempt was enough, however, to instil in the first men on this continent a healthy respect for the great hunting cat. To them it represented the peak of hunting skill and strength, and they made it a god.

Man had, however, one tool that gave even the great cat pause. He could make fire, which the cat feared. This alone set man above the other beasts of the cat's world, and a mutual respect developed between them.

As the Indian cultures developed, the great cat became more and more woven into their mythology. In the southeast the Cherokees called him Klandaghi, Lord of the Forest. Their next door neighbours, the Creeks, called him Katalgar, Greatest of Wild Hunters. The warrior Chickasaws called him Koe-Ishto, or Ko-Icto, the Cat of God. Even the peaceful Zuñis of the southwest called him Father of Game. It was in this desert region where the height of Indian respect for this lordly creature was shown by the primitive tribes of southern California. When the first Jesuits arrived in this beautiful but arid land, the Indians refused to let them protect their flocks and herds from attacks by the great cats.

The priests could not understand this until they learned that for centuries these primitive people had obtained a very substantial part of the meat in their scanty diet by following the hunting cat and scavenging its kills after the rightful owner had eaten his fill. The condors and vultures led them to the kill, and the cat was their great provider. They were in direct competition with other scavengers for its leavings, and they did not dare molest or interfere with it in any way.

Thus in lower California was the great hunter of the mountains and plains the Lord of Creation, and man was relegated to the lowly role of playing jackal to the tiger. I have myself lived on lion kills for a period in Africa, in competition with the other scavengers, and know just how they felt when strangers interfered with the meat supply.

Farther to the south the great cats came into contact with the ancient civilizations of the Mayas of Central America and the Incas of Peru. The Incas listed the puma as a dangerous predator of their herds of guanacos and vicuñas and turned out the army to carry on great ring hunts to exterminate them. This is the first attempt by man to wage systematic war on the species, and is therefore perhaps the first attempt at game management in the New World. Cubs were captured and kept in zoos for the pleasure of the nobles, and some may have been trained for use in war. They were also used as the Romans used the lion against the early Christians, and were kept in dungeons where victims were thrown to them as punishment.

In the north the first European settlers landing on the Atlantic seaboard met the forest-hunting cats, and were reminded of the Asiatic leopard, another name for which is the "panther." It was natural therefore for them to name the solid-coloured cat they met along the deer trails of the Atlantic coastal plain "panther." The illiterate soon contracted this to "painter," and so it has remained ever since, east of the Mississippi. In the northeast it became "The Cat of the Mountain," which in turn was contracted to "catamount," while at the extremity of its range in Maine and New Brunswick it became "The Indian Devil" to the early settlers, which was soon just plain "Injun Devil." The Micmacs of the coasts of the Maritimes called it the "Lhoks,"[1] and the Malecites of the St. John River called it "pi-twal, the long-tailed one."[2] The Penobscots of Maine called it the "lunxus."[3] In the days of the French régime an animal called the "carcajou" appears in the literature. There is some confusion whether the animal referred to is the panther or the wolverine, which was given this name further west.

As the mountainmen pushed across the plains and reached the Rockies of the western United States, the name "mountain lion" begins to appear, and so it is still called in this region. To the north in Canada the animal became the "cougar." In the Spanish-speaking southwest it was "el león" to distinguish it from "el tigre," the jaguar. In South America it is sometimes called "puma." Thus we see that the great cat, the same animal to all but a systematist, is called many names in various parts of its range, yet no one has been able to distinguish positively between skins from the various regions.

In North America east of the Mississippi, the name panther should be used to distinguish the two recognized subspecies that inhabit this region from the thirteen other subspecies recognized in North, Central and South America. The panthers are *Felis*

[1] Adams, A. Leith. 1873. *Field and forest rambles with notes and observations on the natural history of eastern Canada.* London. Henry S. King and Co., p. 58.
[2] Paul, Peter. LL.D. Malecite Indian, June 4, 1970. Pers. com.
[3] Thoreau, Henry David. 1950. *The Maine woods.* Arranged with notes by Dudley C. Lunt. W. W. Norton and Company, Inc. New York, p. 111.

*concolor couguar*, Kerr, from the northeast, and *F. c. coryi*, the Florida Panther, from the southeast. They at one time undoubtedly overlapped in range, and they may still do so occasionally.[4]

The panther was well-known to the settlers along the Atlantic seaboard as far north as New Brunswick. In the days of mature forests and inviolate wilderness, moose and caribou were the principal big game animals of this province. They were heavily preyed upon by wolves, but the panther was so rare a straggler into their haunts that it was of no significance. The white-tailed deer, the panther's mainstay, just reached this marginal range, as there were vast areas of much superior deer range to the west and south.

Then came the settlers. In the mid-Atlantic region they pushed through the centre of the original panther range to the edge of the plains. At the same time in the north the lumbermen and settlers were removing some of the mature forests of Maine and the Maritime provinces as fast as they could with axe, saw and fire. Deer were almost exterminated in many parts of the central portion of the panther's range, and greatly depleted in the rest as the forests disappeared. However, the cutovers of the north, growing up after the removal of the original forest, offered them a haven and a refuge that they were not long in accepting. Soon deer and panthers were evident again in parts of the northeast where they had not been seen in living memory.

Today the wolves are gone south of the St. Lawrence, and the last of the caribou have retreated to a mountain in the Gaspé. Moose have peaked and declined and are now recovering again, and the white-tailed deer is the dominant big game animal of the whole region. Scattered among them are a few family groups of shy, secretive panthers who have learned all there is to know about keeping out of man's way. These panthers are the rarest and least known of the native animals of North America today. They are the survivors of a race that was long thought to have followed the great auk, the Labrador duck, the passenger pigeon, and the sea mink to the end of the trail.

[4] One point that should be cleared up right at the beginning is this: Lions have cubs, tigers have cubs, leopards have cubs, jaguars have cubs, and even cheetahs have cubs. Pumas have cubs in South America, and only the North American mountain lions have "kittens." Throughout this book *Felis concolor* of eastern North America will be called a panther, which name has a long priority, and these panthers will have cubs like all other big cats.

9

To show how the eastern panther has survived in the forests of New Brunswick, and trace its development to today requires a brief historical survey. I have divided the province into ten ranges.[5]

The sheer volume of over 300 sightings is too much to attempt to give in detail. The major incidents will be given in full but the majority will be found in tabular form in Appendix I. The method of procedure will be to circle the great forest in a clockwise direction, starting in the southwest.

The Southwest Range, the Base Gagetown area and the Western Range are continuous from south to north, but are all separated from the main forest by the settlements of the St. John Valley, and are therefore here considered as distinct ranges. The other areas are merely sectors of the perimeter of the great forest, and are considered individually for convenience. The human populations of these various sectors are separate and distinct for geographical reasons, but the panthers, with their internal lines of communication, can move freely from one sector to the other.

Membertou, the Grand Sagamore of all the scattered bands of Micmac and Malecite Indians that inhabited what are now the Maritime provinces of Canada, sat among the elders of the bands planning a raid against the tribes to the south. He thought long, and they waited respectfully as became his great age and experience. At last he spoke.

"We will go in our canoes three days' paddle to the south far out at sea where only the porpoises will see us. We will strike in the dark like the Lhoks, sudden and sure. Then we will be gone back into the dark and the fog before they can assemble against us." The story of "the Lhoks" is the subject of this book.

The next time we may, or may not, have heard of this animal was in a report of a voyage of exploration made by a Frenchman called Diereville in 1708. He travelled from Quebec to Fort La Tour (Saint John) via the St. John River, reporting on the prospects of the country in furs and the possibilities for settlement. He was told by the Indians that the country contained three kinds of animals that he listed as *"chats, loups cerviers, et chats sauvages"*[6]—cats, lynx and wild cats. But by *"chats sauvages"* did

[5] These are clearly indicated on the map.
[6] Diereville, Sieur de. 1708. *Relation du voyage du Port Royal de l'Acadie, ou de la Nouvelle France*. Rouen.

11

he mean bobcats or racoons? The racoon was called a *"chat sauvage"* by the French in Ontario.[7]

Then came a man called Cooney in 1832. He was a promoter of land sales in New Brunswick and was by no means a naturalist. He described a rather wonderful animal that appeared to have been part wolf, part wolverine and part panther.

Later still was the account of Abraham Gesner, in 1847. He spent most of his time on the north and east coasts of New Brunswick, the poorest panther country in the province. Yet he tells us the *"Felis concolor* panther, painter or catamount—better known in the Province as the Indian Devil—although small, is a very dangerous animal: They are very rare, yet sometimes a single skin is brought into the market [at Saint John]."[8]

This is the first mention of the two names panther and Indian Devil in the literature of this region.

Thirty-seven years later the Natural History Society of New Brunswick published its first mammal list in 1884. It lists the animal as follows: "1. Panther. No recent instances known."

Then came Boardman, the naturalist of the St. Croix, whose region was and still is the best panther country in the province. He recorded the animal as "well-authenticated"[9] in 1899.

He was followed in 1903 by Ganong who was the first scientist to see and record observations in the central part of the province. He could find "not a solitary authentic record, or any other authentic evidence, of either the present or former occurrence of the panther within the limits of New Brunswick."[10]

By these four names, the "Lhoks," "Pi-Twal the long-tailed one" and the "Lunxus" of the Indians, and the Indian Devil of the early settlers, was the largest of North American cats first known in the northeastern part of the continent. Today we have given this almost mythical beast a Latin name. We call it *Felis concolor couguar*, Kerr, although the validity of the subspecies inhabiting eastern Canada is suspect because not enough specimens have been examined to verify it.

---

[7] Clarke, C. H. D. 1969. "The Puma in Ontario." *Ontario Fish and Wildlife Review.* 8(4) Winter. pp. 7-12.

[8] Gesner, Abraham. 1847. *New Brunswick* (including a catalogue of mammals). London. Simmonds and Ward.

[9] Boardman, G. A. 1899. "St. Croix mammals." *Calais Times.* Calais, Maine. Nov. 23 reprint. The Naturalist of the St. Croix, S. L. Boardman. Bangor, Maine. 1903. pp. 319-21.

[10] Ganong, W. F. 1903. "On reported occurrences by the panther *Felis concolor* in New Brunswick." Bull. Nat. Hist. Soc. N.B. 21. 82-6.

Gradually the animal disappeared with the settlement of the country, and was finally listed as extinct. But as the lumber and pulpwood industries developed and removed the remaining mature forests of the region, the second and third generations of trees grew up to take their place. The mature forest had supported moose and woodland caribou, but very few white-tailed deer. For this reason the panther was always scarce there as deer are its preferred food. With the development of the second and third growth forests the region changed from a moose and caribou ecology to a deer ecology, and consequently the few panthers thrived and multiplied.

There were scientists in the region now and they were not satisfied with the colloquial names of Indian Devil, catamount, painter, and others applied to the animal in different regions in early days. They called it the panther and gave it a Latin name. This was many years before the western names of mountain lion and cougar came into common use. Today the name panther is the common name used for both the northern and southern subspecies east of the Mississippi River, and the names mountain lion and cougar are used for the western subspecies. How valid these subspecies are lies in the realm of the old argument between the splitters and the lumpers. The same basic animal is found today from the Yukon to Patagonia, and once more from the Atlantic to the Pacific.

So matters stood for thirty-five years. Boardman said the animal was well-authenticated in his area and Ganong said there was no authentic evidence of the presence of the animal in the province, and never had been. Then in 1938, when I was a member of the Fire Hazard Research Division of the Dominion Forest Service, I was working on a fire in northern New Brunswick.

The wind had changed and the fire was sweeping through a new stand. My companion had just finished regrouping his fire fighters and we were eating lunch.

"Did any game come out when the fire reached this stand?"

"No, but the foreman saw a panther moving ahead of the fire this morning."

I was too amazed to reply.

As far as I knew the nearest panther, cougar or mountain lion was in the Rockies of Alberta. When I queried him he replied, "Oh yes. We have them here too, but they are very rare. I shot one myself when I was a boy in Maine."

From then on all other wildlife of the region took a backseat for me. I would find a panther.

I had forgotten that someone had told the world there were panthers surviving in New Brunswick long after they were regarded as extinct in the northeast. He was a competent woodsman who had travelled all over the wilder parts of New Brunswick, and was one of the foremost animal writers of his day—Sir Charles G. D. Roberts.

One of his short animal stories, "The Watchers of the Camp Fire," is the story of a panther born on the sources of the Naskwaak that wanders to the headwaters of the Upsalquitch. It heads westward "into deer country" and follows the trail of a lone man on snowshoes. It finds him bivouacked in the snow. It watches him closely as his fire dies down and he goes to sleep. A young doe is attracted by the flickering light of the fire and approaches. The panther sees her and immediately starts to stalk the animal, forgetting the man. He awakes and shoots the panther.

This little tale, written in New Brunswick before 1902, is so perfectly typical of the behaviour of a panther, recorded many times since in the west, that it strongly suggests it is based on an actual incident. There are other references and drawings of "the Northern panther," as Sir Charles calls the animal, scattered through his writings of the New Brunswick back country.

However, the accepted scientists of the day were of little help. Opinions seemed to be evenly divided. When you have finished this book you can form your own opinion.

The following accounts of panthers in the northeast are based upon an assumption for which there is no positive proof. It is that when a series of reports comes in from an area within a limited period of time they all refer to either the same animal, the same pair of animals, or the same mother with her cubs. This assumption is based on the obvious fact that this is an extremely rare animal and if each report represented a different animal they would be so numerous that they would leave abundant signs such as tracks and kills. Anyone who has spent fruitless days searching for signs in an area from which several reports of panthers have come will appreciate the validity of this assumption.

# Chapter 2
# The panthers
# of eastern Canada

New Brunswick

The Southwest Range

In this range, the southwest corner of the province, the panther
has been known for a long time. This is Boardman's country.
Time and again the woodcutters came to this rough land and cut
out the saw logs and later the smaller trees for pulpwood. In
their wake had spread swift-running wildfire, and soon most of
the area was a patchwork of burns growing up with young trees
of different ages. This was ideal for moose and deer.

In June 1944, one of the panther family there was caught
in a ridiculous situation. Three men were fishing at the
mouth of Porcupine Lake from a canoe. They heard a noise
"like the water injector on a steam engine" coming from behind
the fringe of flooded alders along the shore. This was accompanied by splashing, as if some heavy animal were jumping in
the water. Quietly they paddled up to the alders and the man in
the bow stood up.

Mr. Nixon saw "An animal as large as a man, the colour of
a deer, and with a long tail, standing on its hind legs in the
water. . . . We thought it was chasing frogs by standing on its
hind legs to spot them and then pouncing. That was the splashing we had heard. When it saw us it dropped to all fours and
made off slowly without any haste and apparently unfrightened.
. . . ." The panther disappeared into the alders, salvaging as much
of its dignity as it could by growling sulkily to itself as it watched
the excited men arguing about what they had seen.

One December evening an eleven-year-old girl and her uncle were skating on a small lake on the Gooseberry Cove Road. It was a beautiful moonlit night and they were just beginning to enjoy themselves when the female panther called loudly and imperiously from the heavy spruce swamp behind the lake.

The wild fierce scream of the panther to her mate terrified the child and she began to cry. Her uncle was frightened too, not knowing the source of the strange call. As soon as the child began to cry the panther answered and started to approach her. The child and her uncle fled precipitously, without stopping to remove their skates, leaving the disgruntled panther making twelve- and fifteen-foot leaps in the snow trying to find who had answered her mating calls. She never did—but a man and a girl will never forget her voice. As the child's mother put it, "I don't think any of us down this way desire to cultivate a closer acquaintance with these gentle 'Indian Devils'."

It was in July of 1945 that the female ventured close for a good look at man. Four men were sitting down eating their lunch after working hard all morning, cutting and peeling pulpwood. A freshly-peeled log lay beside them as they munched their sandwiches and smoked. Suddenly one man jerked his head up and pointed. A female panther was standing on the far end of the peeled log watching them curiously. She walked the length of the log never taking her eyes off the men.

"That's close enough!" one said, and hurled a stone at her. It missed and she watched it fall before stepping off the log and disappearing into the bush, leaving four astounded men gazing after her.

It was the following winter before the big male showed himself. He was crossing West Long Lake on the ice as he had done at intervals all winter, and he had long since given up bothering about staying under cover in daylight. There had not been a man on the lake for two months, and he moved freely whenever he wanted.

He was walking slowly across the ice in his slouchy, completely relaxed fashion, when he came to fresh snowshoe tracks up the lake. He sank to his haunches and smelled them, and then bounded for the shore in long leaps. The great tail held out behind was in marked contrast to the sinuous "swish, swish" from side to side of its limp counterpart as he sauntered along at ease. He did not know it, but he had been seen by the maker of the snowshoe tracks from behind the trees on shore, and the word that the Injun Devil was still there was passed along.

On "the day of the big storm" in early February 1948, Joe Beck and his wife and two sons were at their farm in Central Blissville. One son was just leaving the house to go back to work after lunch when he called out: "Come and see these!"

Two panthers, a large one followed by a smaller one, came out of the woods and crossed the farm at a dead run. The next day another, or one of the same pair, appeared at about the same time and followed the same trail across the farm. That night a deer was killed and eaten, leaving nothing but the skin and leg bones on the main road. After this the panthers were not seen all the following summer.

On December 22nd, 1948, near Vespra Siding on the main C.P.R. railway track, Winford Webb had the experience of his life. He later reported: "I spent the day at my hunting camp at Vespra and at dusk on the evening of December 22 I left camp and proceeded to the railway tracks to walk east four miles to Tracy . . . and I was alone at the time. . . . I heard the wire fence rattle on the south side of the railroad tracks. I stopped and listened but saw nothing further until with one graceful bound he leaped on to the track broadside to me. . . . I would estimate that from the tip of his nose to the tip of his tail he was eight feet long. I make this estimate as he nicely covered the standard eight-foot ties . . . his face was like an overgrown cat with extra long whiskers. He made no attempt to attack me or snarl. . . . I did not have any weapon. He with another leap, with seemingly no effort on his part, landed on the north side of the track. Without any run at all, the next leap was over the eight-foot wire fence with plenty of clearance at the top. . . ."

He estimated the animal that cleared that eight-foot fence with such ease weighed 150 pounds or more, so it was undoubtedly the big male.

In August 1950, one of the cubs was swimming the Digdequash River. It had reached midway when a canoe with two men in it rounded a bend and saw it in midstream. The cub paused with only its head and the tip of its tail showing, staring at the canoe which it had never seen before. Then, as this strange creature remained at a respectful distance, it resumed its crossing and mounted the far bank in a slow dignified walk. Just before it disappeared into the bush it allowed itself a long steady stare.

The old male had long since lost his eye-stripes. He was in his declining years, and it had been a rather wonderful life. Man had not troubled him in any serious way, and all the food he wanted was there for the taking. He had watched men innumerable times without being seen, and on a very few occasions they had watched him. His feelings toward them were respectful but neutral, and he avoided them scrupulously.

In this frame of mind he met the Manager of the Bank of Nova Scotia at St. George, New Brunswick.

It was a hot day in August 1953, and the big male had stretched out on a great expanse of flat rock he had found, soaking up the morning sun. As the heat increased he moved off the rock into the shade. He had been lying on the abandoned runway of a deserted airfield. He heard a car arrive somewhere in the distance out of sight, and shortly after he saw a strange bird overhead.

It zoomed and dived and finally it plunged into the bush. Soon he heard excited voices and a man and boy came searching along the edge of the old runway. At once the panther took cover.

The man and the boy had been flying a model airplane, and they were seeking it after its last flight. It had landed on the opposite side of the runway from the panther and he watched curiously as they came up. So curious was he to see if they would catch this strange bird that he forgot all caution and stepped out onto the runway in full view to watch. The man and boy froze, gulped, and stared at the great cat just fifty feet away. The panther stared back. Then quietly, and with dignity, he turned around slowly and withdrew out of sight.

A few nights later the man and his son saw the Disney nature film "Bear Country" showing the mountain lions, and there was no further question about what they had seen at the old airfield. The bank manager called the Wildlife Station to report a panther that night.

The big male was very alert now, and he allowed no close approaches if he was warned in time. However, a cub was not so

18

lucky. In the same month it had followed the deer into the orchard of Hugh Purdy at The Ledge. Hugh was well aware of the attractions of his orchard for deer, and this evening at dusk he was sitting quietly with his back to one of the trees with a 16 ga. shotgun loaded with slugs across his lap.

The squirrels and the birds played overhead and gave their evening calls as the light died. Just as it was getting too dark to see, the birds and squirrels suddenly became silent. Into the orchard stepped a young panther. It stood broadside to Hugh at fifty yards and offered a perfect shot. The shotgun roared and ripped a hole clean through the animal with blood and hair falling two feet beyond.

It reared, bit at its flank, and was lost in the shadows in a single bound. In the last of the light Hugh did not follow. He went home and went to bed, and the following day he worked all day before he was free to return to the orchard. There he found more blood but could follow no trail, and again he went home disappointed.

Amid the large crevices of the tumbled rocks behind the orchard fence a pair of fierce yellow eyes closed for the last time that night. The cub died and was forever lost amid the deep cracks in the river rocks. Its sepulchre was sealed by the snow that covered the land two days later. Thus was lost to man another of the almost legendary Injun Devils of New Brunswick.

In February 1958, the female came into heat. When her passion reached its peak she followed her mate's cold trail out into the fields of Fred Weeks on the Oakhaven Road. Savage calls broke from her as she puzzled out the cold trail, and Fred and his wife stood on the porch and watched her light red coat with the darker shoulders glinting in the bright sun as she coursed over the snow. After about five minutes she passed on into the woods leaving them with an unforgettable experience.

The following month came the first report of an unusual coloured specimen in the district. On a gravel side road, a few miles past Chamcook, a car was moving slowly along the rough surface. Its sole occupant, J. D. MacDonald, saw a large cat with a long tail standing beside the road. It turned to look at him for several seconds, then sprang into the bushes and disappeared. He described it like this.

"The animal was quite definitely black, and my first thought was that it was a panther. . . ." The time was 3:00 p.m. It . . . "may have been about three feet long, not counting the tail."

It was not a full-grown adult, which suggests that a black cub was born in the region about 1959. Was it the result of the chase Mr. and Mrs. Weeks watched on February 18, 1958?

It may well have been, as the female had one well-grown normal- coloured cub with her when she stepped out on a woods road seventy-five yards ahead of Frank McIntyre of Lawrence Station on August 17, 1961. She and the cub stood and looked at him before walking unhurriedly away around the bend. The next day he returned with a forest ranger who made plaster casts of their tracks. The cub was about as large as a redbone hound: that is, small enough to be the runt of the litter that had just broken up and was still clinging to its mother. McIntyre, who had fifty years experience hunting in the region, had never before seen the panthers, although he had heard of them many times.

This was the first mention of a black individual seen in the area, and it appeared at intervals thereafter as we shall see.


On October 15, 1962, a female was lying in the morning sun beside a boulder, toying with the remains of a beaver she had killed and eaten several days before. She was of the grey colour phase, and as light fell on her coat it gave her a bluish-grey tinge. She was therefore a different animal from the one seen by the Weeks in 1958.

She became alert as she heard the approach of two deer hunters. When they came into sight she rose, and, leaving her beaver, walked off into thick cover. Miraculously neither hunter raised his rifle. They stared excitedly after her and one collected the teeth of the beaver as a souvenir; then they resumed their hunt.

In mid-afternoon they shot a deer and dragged it to the highway. As they sat resting, the big male panther stepped out on the highway from his hiding place 100 yards away and stood staring at them. They approached to within thirty yards of him.

"I could have shot it with a shotgun," one hunter affirmed afterwards.

The animal stared at them, and then turned and walked slowly away up the highway. When a car approached he stepped off into the bushes to let it pass, but then returned to the road walking slowly along until he was lost to sight.

Why did the men not shoot? Because they were Canadian soldiers who had never hunted in New Brunswick before, and they had just returned from a tour of duty in Germany where they had been very impressed with the strictness of the game laws and the seriousness with which they were enforced. It never occurred to them that these apparently unfrightened animals had every reason to dread them. They took it for granted these magnificent creatures were protected.

They knew at a glance that the smaller grey female and the big tawny male seen later were different animals (the track of the latter was "wider than my fist"), and they found some old deer bones where the big male stepped out on the pavement. He had been lying watching one of his deer crossings when the hunters arrived dragging their deer, and he moved off at the disturbance.

The soldiers reported their experience to the Royal Canadian Mounted Police, and only then did they learn that the panthers were unprotected. At the Wildlife Station the biologists heaved a sigh of relief and crossed their fingers. The panther pair would not survive another encounter with armed men if they acted in this naïve fashion again.

At seven o'clock in the evening of June 28, 1963, Mrs. D. J. Scarratt and Miss Sue Corey, both biologists of the Atlantic Biological Station of the Fisheries Research Board of Canada, were driving toward St. Andrews on Route #1. At the junction of the Fiander Road with Route #1 a full-grown panther came out of the bush on the inland side of the road and paused briefly in the centre of the pavement to look at the car. Then it walked off the road and out of sight on the seaward side.

One week later, and at almost the same time, Dr. D. J. Scarratt and his wife were again driving toward St. Andrews on Route #1. At the junction of the Fiander Road Mrs. Scarratt said to her husband, "This is where we saw the cougar last week."

"When she was in mid-sentence, as though the animal had been listening, a cougar came out of the bushes in almost the same place as the previous week and crossed the road and entered the bushes again on the seaward side. Needless to say this was quite exciting. The body of the animal I would judge to be about four feet long, with a tail as long or nearly as long. The colour was a tawny grey and the very tip of the tail appeared to be blackish. There is absolutely no question in my mind as to the identity of the beast."

What was the lure that brought the big male to the tidewaters of the Bay of Fundy at the same place twice in the period of a week? His relatives on the shores of the Strait of Magellan in far-off Patagonia hunt the beaches for sea lion pups, and there are harbour seals on the rocks and beaches of St. Andrews. Was the big male at the northern extremity of the hemisphere-spanning range emulating his cousins at the southern extremity?

Two months later, on August 27, 1963, the big male again pushed his disregard of people to the point where only pure luck saved him from being shot.

On this date he had followed a deer and tried to intercept it for some hours. He was very hungry as he had not eaten in several days, but he had missed his first rush and the deer was fully alerted. Still he stayed with it, and it led him to a low thicket 300 yards behind Rubie's Restaurant, about a mile west of St. George. It was 7:30 p.m. when he located the deer in the thicket, but the light was still good.

There were several people about the restaurant out at the highway as he crossed the field, but he ignored them. However, his passing was not unnoticed. C. Gordon Noble describes the incident thus.

"My attention was drawn by a stranger to what he called a cougar, and naturally I laughed at him before looking.

"However, he was right. Directly across the field three or four hundred yards away was what could not have been anything but a panther. He appeared to be stalking another animal, which must have been in a low thicket. I called Mr. Thorne, the proprietor of the place, and by the time he came out, saw the panther, went back to his home and returned with his rifle, the panther had disappeared in the thicket. In the meantime a couple of bystanders had gone after it and were throwing rocks into the thicket. One of them either hit or made a near miss, as the panther burst out of the thicket in a rush and made for the woods. I never saw an animal travel like that."


The Western Range

To the north of the last region, between the St. John River and the Maine border, lies the lake country of New Brunswick. This

22

is the most westerly panther region in the province, but to a panther it is no doubt continuous with the eastern Maine areas, except where a chain of large lakes separates them. It too has been the home of panthers for many years.

"A large feline animal" attacked and seriously injured a man near Fredericton in 1841. It was reported to Staff Surgeon-Major A. Leith Adams in 1873 by one of my predecessors, Dr. Robb, Professor of Natural History at the University of New Brunswick, who also stated that he had seen the skin of a puma from the vicinity of Quebec.

At the turn of the century a farmer at Springhill above Fredericton found signs of a panther about his pasture where he had some sheep and young cattle. He set a bear trap and caught it. When he returned to his trap he had no gun, or even an axe to dispatch the captive. When he approached, it bared its teeth, snarled at him and spat. He was alone, and he was a courageous man. He went to the fence and took a fence rail and with this crude weapon he slew the trapped cat.

The skin was preserved as a rug for many years where it was seen by a small boy who is now the retired Curator of Natural Science at the New Brunswick Museum. He particularly remembers that the tail was at least two feet long, and the hide was tan-coloured without spots.

In April 1904, about forty miles to the northwest, a panther gave an exhibition of fearlessness that two men will never forget. F. H. McGivney and his father were sugaring two miles east of Pickard Ridge west of Pokiok. Their camp was about a mile from another, and they used to whoop to each other at night when the sound carried best.

This night young McGivney whooped, but he got an answer from another direction. He whooped at intervals and got an answer each time. Whatever was answering was coming toward him. He at first thought it was one of the men from the other camp who had been lost and was making his way to their camp. A large animal approached through the trees. It had a heavy-shouldered body three and a half feet long with a long, heavy tail that was not bushy. His father recognized it at once as a panther.

It approached to within 200 feet of their fire, but would come no closer. It growled and leaped from tree to tree and seemed very excited. The cry it gave began with a deep growl and built up to a shrill whooping scream.

They were both considerably frightened although they had a gun. They did not dare fire at it, and stayed up all night. It stayed around for several hours and finally left just before daylight.

Sixteen years later, in the fall of 1920, the panther family west of Pokiok was heard from again. Two deer hunters set out after supper to bring in a deer they had shot that afternoon. They had about two miles to go over a hardwood ridge. The late Edward Pugh of the New Brunswick Game Department told me the story.

"We first heard a snarl directly ahead and at short range, followed shortly afterwards by a loud yowl. This call was answered from about a mile away by a second animal. This animal called at intervals as it approached until the two met.

"They followed us home, one behind and the other on the side, and came very close on several occasions. My brother and I were considerably frightened although we had rifles, as the animals kept just beyond the range of the light and kept up a continuous loud yelling. . . . These animals sounded very much louder and stronger than a bobcat or a lynx, with the cries of which I am familiar. We did not get the deer that night."

On March 1, 1941, a large panther deliberately sat in a hauling road as a team of horses pulling a heavy load of logs came around the bend. The plodding team came to within twenty-five yards before they noticed it. The horses shied as the teamster stared, but the panther showed no fear. It finally walked off the road with a slinking gait that reminded the teamster of a pacing horse. The man estimated its head was four feet from the ground when sitting down, and standing it was two and a half feet high and three and a half feet long excluding the tail, which was long and carried like a house cat's.

Its coat was a mixture of yellow-grey and reddish, and the length of the hair was such as to make the neck appear to be thicker than the head. As the man sat looking at the fearless yellow eyes regarding him, and trying to regain control of his terrified team, he remembered that a friend had told him of following the panther's trail and finding where it had chased a bobcat up a

24

tree, caught it, and eaten it in the tree. His friend had brought back pieces of the bobcat.

In September of 1946 a female had just killed a deer between Second and Third Eel Lakes, and it had been quite a struggle. The deer had jumped a second before her charge got home, and the panther had missed the lethal neck grip. They had rolled and thrashed about until she finally got the grip she wanted and her canine teeth sank into the deer's vertebrae to end the struggle. It had been an all-night hunt and dawn was just breaking when she finally made the kill.

She had just started her meal when she heard men approaching. Loath to leave, she lingered at the carcass until the last minute, and then climbed a tall maple nearby. Three deer hunters entered the clearing and stood staring at the slain deer. They soon found the large cat tracks.

The panther settled comfortably on her branch and watched curiously as the men cut branches and built a blind with a good view of the kill.

By four in the afternoon they had seen nothing and were both stiff and cold. They decided to come back the next day and bring a trap, and before leaving Sandy McArthur walked over to the kill for a final look around. For some reason he glanced up into the big maple——and looked squarely into the eyes of the panther.

"All we could see was his glistening eyes and part of a back. He was lying parallel with the limb and watching us. I could have killed it with a .22, but Virgil's shot must have gone through its hair. That animal left the branch and, like an acrobat, he came to the ground on all fours. But we both saw the huge tail without any question. This animal was large and the head was not too small. The small space of time I had to watch it I noticed its very bright eyes that really seemed to burn."

They returned the following day, but little of the carcass was left and it had been moved into heavy cover. There were lots of "small tracks about it in addition to the large ones." Was a female naïve enough to bring a litter of small cubs back to a kill that had been found and where she had been fired at? But how else would the carcass of a full grown deer disappear overnight?

In May or June of 1948, an incident occurred near York Mills, York Co., New Brunswick which I was able to check personally

some time later. The delay was caused by the fact that the victim was so badly frightened that he left his job, and it took a year to find him again. Ephraim Michaud was a pulpwood cutter and he left his saw and went down to the brook for a drink. He was lying flat on his face drinking when an animal jumped on his back. It fastened its teeth in his right shoulder but let go at once when he struck back with his elbow.

He scrambled to his feet and got his back against a tree. It came at him again and struck out with its paw clawing him across his right side down to the groin. He turned away to protect his stomach and it clawed him down the back ripping his shirt. Whereupon he turned and kicked it hard three times in the flank and stomach and it made off. He was bleeding freely and his shirt was almost torn off when he reached the Little Camp where he was employed. He was taken to Harvey where his wounds were dressed by a nurse. Nothing would induce him to return to work in the area, and he left.

A year later I found him in another camp. His wounds had healed. He described the animal that attacked him as brown in colour with a long tail, six feet overall. He picked out the picture of a mountain lion in Nelson's *Wild Animals of North America* without hesitation as his assailant, although he did not know its name.

This incident has all the attributes of a case of mistaken identity. The panther found the man flat on his face drinking from the brook. It apparently only realized it had seized a man after he reared back and stood up. It let go after the initial bite. The subsequent clawing was the natural reaction of suddenly finding itself at close quarters with its most dreaded foe. However, the incident stands as an unprovoked attack on man.


Hazen T. Gorman saw a panther 300 feet ahead as it jumped off the road. He drove up to the place where it disappeared and stopped.

"The cat was in from the road approximately 25 feet. It stared directly at me . . . its head and shoulders were only visible to me, the remainder of the body was obscured by undergrowth . . . the colour of the head was golden. Its head was noticeably small compared to the remainder of the body."

He fired a .22 automatic pistol at its left front shoulder. It disappeared without a sound and he found no evidence that it was hit. It was four years before anybody saw a panther in this region again.

At last on July 15, 1955, a man and his wife were rounding a bend on this same road when they saw a panther standing in the road ahead. It stepped off as they came on, and they stopped where it had entered the ditch. The man got out and gathered stones to throw into the bush to make it show itself. Suddenly the wife saw the panther lying in the bush only five feet away from her husband. He hurriedly reentered the car, and they both watched as it got up and walked slowly away with frequent glances back at them. When the man discovered it at such close quarters it snarled at him and lashed its tail, but as soon as he retreated it showed no further signs of aggression.

Two years later in mid-summer we received a fascinating glimpse of the family life of this group. M. I. Kinney described it thus: ". . . they were what seemed to me quite dark in colour, bluish-grey possibly, with very large tails, and were quite heavy set through the head and shoulders. These animals appeared to me to be fighting or having a rough game of play. They were about thirty feet in front of me and stayed there for about two minutes, during which time they were using each other rough. They finally rolled off the road into the ditch . . . and I proceeded on my way."

Fighting or mating? After this no one saw them for another four years. By which time a litter born from this mating, if such it was, would be independent and well-established on its own ground.

Then in March 1959, the panther became the subject of a special report by the Royal Canadian Mounted Police. Constable D. L. Lynch, R. C. M. P. in charge McAdam Department, reported to his Commanding Officer the following experience which took place the previous fall. When on patrol in a police car, a large catlike animal crossed in front of his headlights showing a long tail dragging behind. Never having heard of panthers in this region at that time, he concluded it must be a bobcat and thought no more about it. Later, when talking to others who had seen the local panthers, he realized this was what he had seen and submitted an official report of the incident.

28

Two sightings followed, almost a year apart, of a very unusual small panther that was black or very dark brown in colour. The first was in the headlights at night at a distance of 100-150 feet. It was described as "black as a bear . . . the picture of ease and grace . . . and about forty pounds in weight." The day before, near the same place, a porcupine was killed by some animal that ate out the carcass down to the skin of the tail and left the skin rolled in a ball with the quills inside.

A year later, on October 29, 1960, a panther was seen at 9:30 a.m. at seventy-five yards by two men. It crossed a main road and a woods road at a slow walk and apparently never noticed their car. They saw it in good light and got a clear view. They described it as having a body three feet long, tail eighteen inches, and sixteen inches at the shoulder. It was either black or very dark brown all over. It had apparently moved into the district to stay for some time.

In July of the following year cat calls "like a baby crying" were heard near Lake George, and a woman startled a large cat lying in some tall grass. It was just at dusk, and she did not see it long enough to give a description, but on August 26, 1961 her husband saw it again at the same place and in daylight. R. S. Miles (P.Eng.) described it: ". . . the animal had a long tail. The forward part . . . appeared to be a grey or tawny colour, while the tail, and I think the hindquarters, were either dark brown or black; more likely, dark brown."

Five days later, and about twenty-five miles away, three boys bicycling to school reported a large black cat lying in the ditch. It was about "the size of a police dog," and it bounded away into the woods when they approached. Later the same day the mother of one of the boys saw it nearby. She telephoned the Fredericton Police who notified the Wildlife Station. Large cat tracks were found where the boys had seen it lying in the ditch.

A local resident's report to me was something of a classic. "Mr. Wright I seen a panther-cat this morning. Black on the back and brown on the sides. Three car lengths away—and JEE-SUS! DID HE HAVE WHISKERS! He come up kind of gant in front of the hind legs. Not like a bobcat."

At McGundy Stream on October 20, 1964, Guide M. McDonald of McAdam was driving two American woodcock hunters. They saw a panther sitting in an open field at 150 yards. They backed up their station wagon and climbed on top of it for a better view. It then got up and ran across the field in full view of them all.

It was "exactly like an African lion" dark in colour, darker than the dead grass on which it sat, "a very dark brown all over." As it ran, its long tail showed clearly. "It was the greatest thrill of my life," McDonald said later.

And here I would like to add my mite to the pile of evidence available. On September 28, 1966, at 2:00 p.m., my wife and I were driving west from Fredericton toward the U. S. border. We were one-half mile east of York Mills, York County, N. B., on the main highway when we rounded a curve. My wife was driving. The light was excellent. We both noticed an animal standing in the right-hand ditch.

The animal stepped up onto the pavement and walked leisurely out to the centre stripe where it stopped broadside, looked toward us, and then moved at a fast walk across the road and up a cut bank into the bush. It was in sight about ten seconds.

We both noted the long tail dropping to its turn-up above the ground. The animal was about as high as an English setter dog, but I thought it was longer. It was the uniform colour of a deer. When it disappeared into the bush it was not more than fifty yards ahead of us. After twenty years of investigating panther reports, photographing and making plaster casts of their tracks, and photographing their kills, I had finally seen a live New Brunswick panther, and, with a witness.

This was another instance of the futility of attempting to take photographs of this elusive beast. As was my habit during the past twenty years, I had a pair of binoculars on the seat beside me and a camera with telephoto lens mounted on the seat behind, with an exposure meter on the dashboard in front. I got as far as getting my sun glasses off before the animal was out of sight. When the first clear picture of the eastern panther is taken in the wild it will not be by a chance encounter on a road, but of a treed animal or from a successful flash trap. On the road the chances of getting a camera into action, no matter how well-prepared one is, are almost nil. The element of surprise is too

30

great, and the duration of the average observation is too short. This was our experience.

In the last week of September 1966, Mrs. Ruth Cleghorn, her husband and two sons were in a field at South Tweedside, York County. They saw a porcupine, and the husband and eldest boy went to kill it leaving the wife and the young boy behind. A panther came out within twenty feet of the pair. It stared at them for a few minutes and leaped away. It was a full-grown adult. There were cattle in the field all summer but it did not molest them. It was fired at when eating a squirrel. It stayed around for about two years and did no damage.

During 1967 panthers were seen in this range on four separate occasions. One is worth telling in some detail. Victor Collett is a tractor operator for the Department of Public Works in Fredericton. He was going to work at 7:50 a.m. on the morning of August 16, 1967. He was working on a construction job on the Hanwell road in York County. A panther sprang out of the woods and crossed the road in front of him in three leaps. Its long tail hit the ground with a thump at the end of each leap. Its head and body were four feet long, and the tail was almost as long again. It was a shiny jet black all over.

"It glittered in the sun, and its hide would make a beautiful pelt."

It was travelling fast and did not stop. Five minutes later a big bobcat crossed in the same place following the panther. The difference between the two was obvious and striking.

Two nights later a man living alone in a camp about 200 yards from the point where the panther had crossed the road was awakened at 10:30 p.m. by a noise in his camp yard. He got up and looked out his window. He saw "a large black animal in the yard. It was five feet long and about two and one-half feet high. I took it for a bear. I was frightened as I had no gun, and scared it away by rattling the stove lids."

He kept his milk in a plastic jug. That night the jug was empty and he hung it in a tree. In the morning it was on the ground and crushed with claw marks, an inch apart, which penetrated the side.

Two months later a black panther was seen by a hunter ten miles away.

31

On April 12, 1970, a black specimen stayed for five minutes in sight of two observers on the outskirts of Fredericton. They whistled at it but it was not alarmed.

On May 25, 1970, Dr. Uno Paim, Professor of Biology of the University of New Brunswick, had a panther cross in front of his car on the Harvey-McAdam road near the Magaguadavic bridge. He stopped his car and followed the animal into the woods. He was about ten paces from it before he saw it. The movement of the black tip of the tail caught his eye. It was a heavy-set, grey-brown animal with a black tip to its long tail. It was gone in a flash.

The Base Gagetown Range

This area is continuous with the Southwest Range to the west but has sufficient information and interest to justify separate treatment. It comprises the west bank of the St. John River from Fredericton to Saint John and is bounded on the west by Route #101 to Wirral, and a line from Wirral to Prince of Wales on Route #1. This is a region of about 800 square miles. More than half of it is the military training area of Base Gagetown.

In the north this region is relatively flat with broad rolling ridges covered with forests and abandoned farms. In the military area the abandoned farms are reverting to forest, and require extensive brush control to maintain the openings. To the south the area rises to the hill massif culminating in Mount Champlain from where the hills run south to the Bay of Fundy. This area is heavily forested over rough rocky terrain and is used as a jungle fighting training area by the Canadian Army.

In the fall of 1953 a panther was wounded but not recovered. On the second day of the deer season, October 2, 1953, a hunter stood watching a deer trail on the high ground behind Grand Bay. After he had been some time at his stand he noticed a panther lying down watching him from behind a bush, eighty yards away. Finally it rose and turned broadside to him, and he fired at it with a 12 ga. shotgun loaded with a slug. It disappeared into some bushes and he thought he had hit it, but he found nothing. He went out for help and he and a companion searched the area thoroughly but found no trace of the animal. He concluded that he must have missed.

Five days later he was again hunting in the area and was about 200 yards from the point where he had fired on the first trip. Suddenly he saw the hindquarters of an animal lying on a log about thirty yards away. The head and forequarters were behind a leafy maple. He watched for some time until it stood up and jumped off the log, clearly showing a long tail. He fired S.S.G. shot at it when it started to move, but shot scars on the tree indicated he had shot high. There was again no blood or hair. I examined the log carefully but it was a smooth-barked hardwood and contained no hair.

Two weeks later another hunter was in the area. About one-quarter mile from where the panther had been seen twice he came to a slashing and stopped to watch. The panther was lying at the base of a stump in the sun. It saw him immediately and stood up. He fired a shotgun slug at it and it was knocked to its knees. However, it recovered at once and made off. He did not fire again or attempt to follow.

When I examined the area twenty days later, the tracks of a medium-sized panther showed fresh in the trail (it had rained the night before). Either there was more than one in the area, or it had survived its wound.

On August 12, 1954, about twelve miles away below Gagetown on the river road, the rural mailman was making his morning run. He was coasting down an incline making a minimum of noise when a panther followed by three others of about the same size came out on the road ahead of him. They were tawny grey-ish, and their fur appeared to be "roughed up." When they saw the car they separated and two went off on one side of the road and two on the other. They were most probably a mother and a full-grown litter of three cubs which were just about to leave her.

The two observations of what appeared to be ragged-coated panthers in 1954 suggest that some disease such as mange may have been prevalent among them at this time.

In early September 1955, the Camp Commandant of Base Gage-town was walking with his dog, a large heavy Chesapeake Bay retriever, along a jeep track at the foot of Blue Mountain. This very steep hill is one of the Mount Champlain massif. They entered an old cutting with the dog running ahead. Lieutenant-Colonel Waugh saw an animal standing at the rear of the cutting at the foot of the mountain watching the dog.

"It was a cat, larger than Pal, black in colour, and with a long catlike tail. My first thought was to get a hold of the dog as if it tackled him he would have no chance. However, as soon as it saw me it ran up the very steep slope at an amazing speed."

The following May two soldiers were returning to Base Gagetown at night when they saw two large green eyes in the headlights. They passed within fifteen feet of an animal standing on the side of the road. Rifleman Steeves, who was nearest, saw ". . . a cat slightly larger than the Colonel's dog, and black in colour. It had a long tail that swished from side to side as we passed."

A month later, on June 17, 1956, a female with a young cub was caught in the headlights of a car in the middle of the Training Area. The driver slowed down when he saw their eyes and stopped within ten feet. They stood and stared at the headlights for three to four minutes and only ran when another car came from the other direction and they were caught between two sets of headlights. The mother was light-coloured, almost yellow, with dark ears. The cub was the size of a fox.

In October 1958, a panther crossed the road in front of a car about a mile from the last sighting. Again the animal was described as "shaggy" which may have indicated that it, too, was afflicted with mange.

A week later a very dark brown, or black, specimen was watched for about a minute by a deer hunter. He put his glasses on it as it crossed an old field, but did not attempt a shot. He made a formal report to the Base authorities on the incident.

A jet black specimen was seen at close range about fifteen miles south of Fredericton. Corporal W. F. Boyd, of the Royal Canadian Corps of Commissionaires was driving west on the Shirley Road and was a mile east of the East Gate of Base Gagetown at 3:45 p.m. The weather was clear and cold, and the visibility was excellent. A panther ran across the road about 100 feet in front of him, and stopped on the side of the bank. It watched the car as he drove up to seventy-five feet and stopped. It remained in sight two to three minutes, giving him ample time to observe it.

It was jet black in colour, with a bluish tinge, and had a light spot on the chest and another near the tip of the tail. The animal was half-grown. It appeared in excellent condition and was "a pretty animal. I have seen a puma in a zoo and this was the same animal," the Corporal reported.

The black specimen caused some mild excitement in Fredericton on June 15, 1962. It was reported by over a dozen citizens to the Fredericton Police as having appeared near a cemetery on the east side of the river. A police alert was put out to the Fredericton and Marysville police to protect the children of the area, but the panther disappeared after doing no damage.

Then came the first report indicating there was more than one black specimen in the area. Corporal Blair Hare, R.C.D., of Base Gagetown, was hunting in the Training Area not far from Blue Mountain where the black panther had watched Colonel Waugh's dog seven years before. He was sitting in a tree with a telescope sighted rifle across his knees watching a field for deer.

A cat walked out into the open and he put his telescope on it. It was a half-grown panther, jet black all over. It crossed the field in plain sight.

Several days later he was back in his tree when another much larger panther with a four-foot body and a tail just as long came out in the clearing and remained in sight for ten minutes. It too was jet black. Corporal Hare watched it through his telescope for the full time it was in sight. He did not fire, as he believed the animal was protected.

There were therefore black specimens in the Base Gagetown area in 1955, and again in 1961-2.

We now come to the first official recognition beyond cursory mention that there are panthers in the forests of New Brunswick. In 1962 the Canadian Army at Base Gagetown undertook a winter exercise called Operation Indian Devil, in an effort to collect a specimen in the Training Area for the Northeastern Wildlife Station. This was carried out by the ski patrols of the Royal Highland Regiment of Canada during the winter of 1962-3. No dogs were used.

On January 29, 1963, Lieutenant Devaney and his patrol were

in the area of Sucker Brook, when they came upon a cat track. It was of small size for a panther and might have been a big bobcat or a lynx. They followed the track on skis and snowshoes, but they had no dog to make the cat tree. However, the track showed definite tail drag, eliminating the bobcat or lynx.

The trail led them to a bed where the animal had been curled up in the snow. They had apparently flushed it from its bed and it had departed as they drew near. The mark of a long thick tail showed plainly in the bed and was photographed by Lieutenant Devaney.

The panther simply walked away from them as they could not travel fast enough to catch up to it. This is another instance of the difficulty of hunting the animal without dogs. The size of the track indicated a young animal or a female. Its tracks were not found again by subsequent patrols, indicating that it was not permanently resident in the area. Further attempts failed to find any fresh sign.

Whether there is any connection or not we do not know, but following Operation Indian Devil there were no more panther reports from the area for four years.


The Central Range

This range covers the home territories of more than one panther family. It is the country lying along the east bank of the St. John River, from Sheffield to the Becaguimec Game Refuge. It is also the region where most effort has been made to trace panther records. It is the closest area to the Wildlife Station, and consequently more information has been available from it than any other region. It is a front of contact between men and panthers along the edge of a large area of almost unbroken forest.

A female panther led her cub along a trail in the rough hills behind Millville one day in the year 1904. She stopped suddenly when she saw a cubby of spruce boughs against the bole of a large tree beside the trail. Her nose twitched as a strange and exciting scent came from it, and her eyes rose to a partridge wing suspended over the mouth of the cubby on a wire, swinging to and fro in the breeze.

She was looking at a trap set which the local trapper, John Gullison, maintained throughout the season along his trapline.

As the panther stood gazing at the set, her eyes on the swaying lure, the inquisitive cub pushed past her and bounded up to seize the waving wing. It caught the wing easily and landed where it was supposed to land, right on the trap.

All that night the cub struggled and the female trod a circle around it. She never dared come within the radius of the trap chain as she had no way of knowing that the strange and terrifying thing that held her cub so remorselessly was now harmless. By noon on the second day the cub had given up struggling and was lying quietly licking its numb paw, while the mother still paced restlessly around in her circle.

Suddenly she paused and listened. With a final small sound to her cub she faded into the shadows and disappeared. Then the cub heard it too. Men were approaching. Gullison the trapper, and his friend David Corey, the game warden from Millville, entered the clearing and stood staring.

Back at Millville none could identify the cub's skin, and it was agreed it must be an Injun Devil. Gullison then sent it to the Hudson's Bay Company for identification. He got a letter back acknowledging its arrival and enclosing a cheque for $3.80 for "the skin of a cougar cub."

Six years later, in 1910, the big male of this family was lying on a boulder overlooking a gully in the rough country at the head of the Nashwaak River. The large yellow eyes became alert as a man came around a bend in the trail and passed on up the gully. He carried a pack and a rifle lay in the crook of his left arm.

The panther slid from his boulder and dropped down to the trail. He would follow this man out of sheer curiosity, making rather a game of it, and never allowing the man to see him. Ahead he heard the sound of chopping, and he circled to get on to the high ground where he could see without being seen. The man was busily constructing a trap set and he never looked up. The panther lay full length behind a log and watched him until he completed the set and adjusted the lure and the scent. Then, picking up his pack, he retraced his steps down the gully.

He had not gone far before he came to the great pad marks of the panther, superimposed on his own tracks. He stood stock still for a long time looking carefully around him, then he continued on his way. But now the rifle was held in both hands across his chest.

Two days later he returned. When he reached his set at the head of the gully he stood staring in amazement. Lying quietly across the mouth of what was left of the cubby, with one paw securely in the trap, was the big male panther. It bared its teeth and spat once as he levelled the rifle. It died without a struggle. The noted New Brunswick author George Frederic Clarke told me: "Burtt Good of Millville trapped a panther on the head of the Nashwaak about 1910. I saw the skin hanging on a wall. The tail was three feet long."

In 1932 a deer hunter was hunting on Little River and was walking along an old woods road. He was just about to cross a good-sized stream when he heard heavy breathing coming toward him. He stepped off into the bushes and a buck deer running full out came down the road, with a large tawny cat with a long tail held straight out behind running just after it. The cat was about eight feet from tip to tip.

When the buck reached the stream it leaped in with the cat following so close behind that the two splashes sounded almost as one. The hunter had a strange rifle with him, "in which he had no confidence," and the size of the cat so impressed him that he tiptoed quietly away in the opposite direction. He never did find out whether the cat caught the deer or not.

On November 2, 1947, a panther lay beside a boulder in a stand of maples on the Nashwaaksis Flats. It was watching a cow and her young calf feeding slowly, about fifty yards away. The cow was oblivious of its surroundings, but everything was new and exciting to the calf.

It would dart to one side to smell some strange object and then lose its nerve and dash back to the cow. This had happened a hundred times that day, and the placid cow now did not even bother to lift its head as the calf came dashing to it. But this time things were different. A six-foot cat, dark red in colour, pounced on the calf and pinned it down. Its pitiful bawl brought up the old cow's head at once, and she turned to face the panther with an angry bellow.

The panther stood with its forefeet on the calf, snarling at the bawling cow, when suddenly a third animal appeared on the scene. A farm dog rushed forward and stopped very quickly when it saw the snarling mask of gleaming teeth ahead. It was then that the panther first noticed the man. He stood thirty feet away regarding the panther with a mixture of awe and disbelief on his face. Man was something it would not face, and it disappeared, moving like a long, low, reddish ribbon, leaving the cow muzzling her unharmed calf. Donald G. Currie reported the incident.

"On the first Sunday in November, 1947, I went out to my sugary to get a cow with a new calf. I heard the cow bawling and went to her. A large animal, dark red in colour, about six feet long, with a striped face, a long tail about twenty-four to thirty inches, and standing about two feet high at the shoulders, had his front feet on the calf watching my dog. I went up to within thirty feet of the animal. It left real fast, going low down. I never could get the dog out to the same place since. I have seen tracks in the snow of this animal at different times. The above is a true statement."

A travelway, where deer and moose, as well as panthers, come out of the swamps about the head of Portobello Stream and pass through the farms to cross the St. John River, is located in Upper Maugerville just below Fredericton.

It was here on January 27, 1948, that a small panther came out of the Portobello swamps and crossed the fields, walking on the snow crust in the middle of the afternoon. The owner of the farm noticed it approaching his barn, and he and his wife watched it through 6x binoculars at a distance of seventy yards. As it neared the houses it lost its nerve and turned back. The farmer then called the Wildlife Station, and we arrived two hours later.

The tracks of a small panther led over the frozen crust along the back of the fields. It seemed to be trying to pass between the farmhouses and reach the river, but each time it lost its nerve and turned back. By this time daylight was fading and we had to give up.

The following morning we were back on the trail and followed it on skis for about two miles. Finally, and probably after dark the night before, it arrived at an old abandoned farm and crawled into the barn. The wind drift in the open had removed all tracks beyond the barn so there was no way of knowing if the animal was still there when we arrived. It required a rather nervous crawl, flat on my back and holding an axe in front of me, through the aperture the cat had used to enter, before I could be sure it was not still present.

An interesting point was that the barn was surrounded by the tracks of domestic cats from the neighbouring farms made that morning. They had apparently all come to investigate the strange scent after its maker had gone.

This panther was travelling, not hunting, as its trail led in a straight line and it showed no interest in other tracks it passed, including those of an otter. It apparently crossed the frozen St. John River during the night and disappeared toward Base Gagetown.

In July of the same year an unusually dark specimen showed itself to two exceptionally well-qualified observers. Dr. D. B. Butterwick, Provincial Veterinary Pathologist, and Dr. J. M. Barette, District Veterinarian, were between the Internment Camp and the Little River Bridge on the Richibucto Road. A full-grown panther crossed the road ahead of their car and stopped on the side of the road to watch them. They drove up to within ten-fifteen yards and stopped the car to observe the animal as accurately as possible. It then bounded up a cut bank and disappeared into the woods. The two professional veterinarians described it as dark brown, almost black in colour; two and a half to three feet at the shoulders; with a "body as long as a full-grown bear," for which it was at first mistaken. From then on there were no sceptics of panther stories in the Veterinary Branch.

On October 29, 1948, Gerald Chute and Arley Marr of Millville were swamping out a road, and had been working all day in the woods. Just as they were about to finish for the day they heard a cry like a man hallooing. They answered and got an immediate reply. Several times they called back and forth and the sound came much nearer. They realized that it was not a man but an animal, and that it was coming toward them.

In a few minutes it stepped out on the new-cut road and they saw it was a panther. They especially noted the long tail. It followed them out to the edge of the clearing and came very close. They arrived at Estey's store in Millville very frightened and took some time to settle down and tell their story. It was obvious that they had been alarmed by what had happened.

It was in November 1949 that the big male came very close to

40

becoming a trophy. A deer hunter and his guide were staying at a camp not far from Marysville. At about eight o'clock on their first evening they heard a scream from nearby that could "best be described as a woman in mortal terror." Another hunter in a camp a mile away also heard the scream and dropped the plate he was washing at the time. A. W. O'Donnell, well-known outdoor writer, who was acting as the guide, said: "Then on Thursday morning I was standing with Mr. R. on the edge of a small clearing, watching for deer. I suggested we return to camp . . . just as we turned to leave I looked back over my shoulder, and there not fifty feet away, stood a large animal. It was slightly crouched and staring at us out of baleful, yellow eyes.

"Mr. R., who is very nervous, fired three times, and it turned and bounded away. As it turned I got a good look at it. It was about five feet in length with a dark tan body, except for the chest which appeared greyish. Its tail was very long and sort of round, and its head was large but not blunt like a bobcat." There was no evidence of a hit, as all three shots went high.

This was a little too much excitement for the nervous Mr. R., and he left for home the next day. A few days later O'Donnell picked up the panther's trail in fresh snow and saw where it followed them right to their camp. It finally disappeared, following a man's track heading north into the big woods and was seen no more that year.

In the early summer of 1952 a female with small cubs was first reported in the district. A large panther with four cubs about twice the size of domestic cats was encountered by two men at Keswick Ridge. It was just at dusk, and although they had a .22 rifle with them, they were badly frightened. They beat a hasty retreat to the edge of the fields, and the large panther followed them all the way. It made no attempt to molest them, but just "saw them off."

Later that year a panther was surprised eating chicken offal by one of these same men. Bruce Duplessis fired at it and knocked it down.

"I got to within twenty feet when it got up and was off like a flash. The long tail was plainly visible on both these occasions."

Then in the early summer of 1953 occurred the first known instance of a panther inflicting actual injury to livestock in New

Brunswick. An interesting coincidence is that it happened to the same farmer, and to a calf of the same cow that had protected her other calf from a panther six years before.

Donald Currie heard the cows bawling in the side hill pasture across the stream, and, shortly afterwards, they all came back to the barn very agitated. Bringing up their rear and moving very slowly was a three-month-old calf of the same cow that had had her calf attacked in that pasture in 1947. Its hindquarters were nearly stripped of hide. It had been grasped by the middle of the back with both paws of an animal with claws, and had apparently pulled away with the claws raking down over the back and hind-quarters to the base of the tail.

When I examined the calf two weeks later (the time it took the report to reach the Wildlife Station ten miles away), the point of the original grip where the claws had dug in deepest was still raw and bloody. The long rakes down the haunches had healed, but no hair had grown on them. Currie thought that the cows had attacked the assailant and driven it off, and this was the bawling that first attracted his attention.

The only other predator large enough to make these wounds would have been a bear, but no bear sign had been seen, and panther tracks had been observed nearly every winter for several years. All the evidence, therefore, pointed to this being a genuine attempt by a panther to kill a calf that was only frustrated by the protection of the herd.

That at least a pair of panthers was in the district was shown a month later by an observation of another farmer about nineteen miles away. He was sitting on his porch when he noticed two large brown animals coming across the field in the direction of his sheep. They were coming at a slow walk. At first he thought they were dogs. He got up and went out to the fence and shouted at them. They passed within fifty yards still at a slow walk. When he shouted again they stopped and looked at him inquiringly.

They resembled lionesses and were brown all over with light yellow faces. They stood considerably higher at the shoulders than his large collie dog, and their tails hung down to the ground, thin and catlike.

He followed parallel to them as they walked across his farm completely ignoring his sheep. They were in sight for at least ten minutes, and disappeared still at a slow walk. They appeared preoccupied with each other and oblivious to outside disturbances, including a man shouting at them fifty yards away. Only a mating pair behave in this way.

On October 16, 1953, a panther created one of the worst scares in the history of the species in the northeast. On October 16, at about 8:30 a.m., children arrived at Birdton school before the teacher. When she came a few minutes before 9:00 a.m., she found them shut in the school and very badly frightened. The younger ones were crying with fear. Shirley White, aged twelve, the eldest child, stated that a large brown animal with a long tail had crossed the front of the schoolyard a few minutes before. It was crouched down, with its belly dragging on the ground, and its mouth open. The children were sure it was going to attack them and ran into the school. It disappeared just before the teacher arrived. None of the now hysterical children could identify the animal.

Four days later the report reached the Wildlife Station and was investigated at once. The animal had been seen across the road from the school again that morning, and the children were again badly frightened. A man with a rifle was keeping watch, and a bus had been secured to take the children back and forth, as all walking to and from the school was forbidden. At the place where the animal was seen that morning the track of a medium-sized panther showed plainly in the mud of the road. It was the track of a young animal which had passed across the school front at a steady walk, paying no attention to the children. Shirley White, who saw it, described it as four feet long with a long tail, and greyish-brown in colour. It slunk along with its belly close to the ground. The teacher was considerably frightened when interviewed, and her husband was standing guard outside with a rifle. When a trailing hound was located and finally brought to the scene several days later the trail was too old to follow.

A month after the event, the story reached the press and lurid headlines blossomed. On November 21, 1953, a month and a day after the panther's last visit to the Birdton school, the *Fredericton Gleaner* trumpeted in half-inch headlines: "PANTHER TERRORIZES CHILDREN IN YORK COUNTY DISTRICT. BIRDTON IS VIRTUALLY BESIEGED TODAY, AS POSSES BEAT THE COUNTRYSIDE FOR TRACE OF PREDATORS."

Two days later *The Toronto Daily Star* joined in with a half-page spread headed: "LARGE 'BLACK DEVIL' PANTHERS, ROAMING THROUGH NEW BRUNSWICK BUSH-LANDS, KEEP SMALL COMMUNITY IN TERROR. CHILDREN SCREAM IN NIGHTS AS PANTHERS TERRORIZE NEW BRUNSWICK VILLAGE.

"Birdton, New Brunswick, November 23 — Fear of the 'Black Devil' panther, a mysterious and terrifying cougar once believed extinct, held this isolated bush community in terror today. Men kept rifles close by and mothers comforted frightened children behind closed doors," the *Star* went on.

Such is the panic-potential of the panther's name, and how easily it can be exploited by a sensationalistic press. Fortunately for all concerned, the young panther that was hunting on the Nashwaaksis stream in the fall of 1953 was not seen again near the Birdton school, and all rapidly returned to normal in the district.

The panther was still in the valley however, for on the day after the *Star*'s story it was seen and fired at by a deer hunter about five miles away. Just at dawn when the mist was lifting the hunter saw what he thought "was a deer standing in a hollow." He worked his way along a log fence to where he had a better view. Here he saw that his "deer standing in a hollow" was "an animal the colour of a deer but much shorter in the legs, with a tail as long as my rifle." He took a quick snap shot as it started to run, but missed. Panther tracks, identical with those from the Birdton school, showed clearly in the mud. It was seen no more in the valley, and its tracks were found heading into the great unbroken forest to the northeast.

The unfortunate experiences at the Birdton school, where the panther had done no damage but had frightened children, awakened all the almost forgotten prejudices against the Injun Devil of grandfather's day. At the Wildlife Station we had to give up, for the moment, talking in public about preserving a rare species.

The following spring a panther carrying a young ruffed grouse in its mouth crossed the road only twenty-five yards in front of a car containing two observers. It was not frightened by the car, and walked slowly along a woods road until out of sight.

At 7 a.m. on June 28, 1955, a panther stepped out on top of a cut bank overlooking a road. It peered cautiously around a clump of grass with only its head showing, but it was spotted by the driver of an oncoming car. The car stopped at once and the man scrambled in the back seat for a rifle.

He levelled a .30-.30 Winchester loaded with hollow-point bullets at the animal's head, and then shifted his point of aim to where he judged the shoulder to be behind the grass. At the shot the panther leaped into the air with a loud catlike screech. When it landed it put its head to the ground and scurried around in a circle biting at one forepaw. The long tail lashed the air in circles, and it made a hissing noise, "like letting air out of a tire," which the man could hear plainly 125 yards away.

He then got back into his car and drove up to where he had last seen the panther, expecting to find it in the ditch. There was nothing there but several spots of bright red blood. Two very hot days later he searched the area thoroughly for two hours looking for a carcass, but without success. A panther with a wounded forepaw roamed the region for the next several months.

That fall a family group had a very narrow escape. Two panthers, as tall as collie dogs at the shoulders, but very much longer, climbed up on a rock pile in Claudie Settlement. They were followed by two cubs about the size of cocker spaniels. A hundred feet away two deer hunters lay watching an orchard.

The large panthers detected the hunters almost immediately and crouched down growling in their direction. The cubs at once took cover. The deer hunters opened up with a barrage of five shots, but at the first the panthers were off like lightning, throwing up large clots of earth behind them. There was no evidence of a hit. Later that night an illegal flashlight swinging across a nearby field spotted all four sets of eyes, so apparently they escaped unscathed.

Two weeks later, and about five miles away, the big male and his mate were trying to corner a deer on Penniac Ridge. The deer knew they were after it and was very alert. Finally, after a night of dodging, it stood out in the open field along the stream where the panthers could not approach. They lay on the ridge above, watching and waiting. As the light grew, a car approached along the road and two hunters in it quickly spotted the deer. They stopped and reached for their rifles, but as soon as the car stopped the deer was off. It reached the woods before either could fire, and the hunters scanned the slope through their rifle 'scopes, watching for it to reappear.

One hunter picked up a reddish animal in his 'scope and fired. It disappeared as a blur in the glass, but his companion saw the deer run from another point on the slope. The animal fired at was long and low and red in colour, and it must have been at least five feet long to have been seen at all.

They crossed to the hill and searched for tracks. In addition to those of the deer they found the tracks of two panthers. I measured the largest. It was five and three-quarters inches across with a twenty-inch stride, deep and heavy. This is the largest track measured so far, but it was made going down a steep hill, and may have been slightly increased by slipping.

In the following year, between July 5 and October 20, 1959, a number of people reported seeing a black panther in the district. On the latter date a hunter on the Claudie Settlement Road (where the other hunters had fired at the family group four years before) saw an animal standing about 200 feet ahead of him. When he first noticed it, the panther was standing between the ruts, but when he stopped it stepped off the road and remained with only its hindquarters showing. He loaded his rifle (a .303 British) and fired through the bushes at where he thought the shoulder would be. It jumped and ran, but he did not think it was hit. It was a small specimen, but "as black as a bear."

The following day the first report of a black specimen came in from the Western Range, as we have seen. It was directly across the river from the site of this encounter. As there are many large islands at this point, a crossing would present no particular difficulty to a badly frightened young panther.

Two months later a panther was followed by the newest menace to this animal's security, the cross-country snow travelling vehicle. Luckily it was a big male on one of his circuits, and not a female on her home territory (a female stays much closer to home than does a male). An experienced bobcat hunter using Bluetick hounds and a Bombardier vehicle cut his trail near Hungry Brook in the Little River Country. The trail ran almost straight for six miles. They followed it twenty-five miles in two days, and then had to give up. Tail drag showed plainly in the trail where it crossed frozen lakes, and the eighteen-inch stride kept on remorselessly mile after mile. When the hunter finally gave up and turned back, the dogs kept on. Four days later, starved and half-frozen, the last of them came out of the woods. We do not know if the big male panther even knew they were following him. He was minding his own business in his familiar surroundings, and he roamed where he chose. Even trail hounds and a cross-country vehicle failed — that time.

For three years after this the panthers did nothing to draw attention to themselves. Then in the spring of 1962 the big male of the Becaguimec country wandered south into the settled area. He was first seen in April, crossing a highway at a distance of fifty yards in good light at 4 p.m. His slow lope gave his observers every opportunity to see him well.

Then on May 13 he gave others a fine view about 9:30 a.m. on a bright clear morning. He strolled leisurely along the main road, jumped the ditch, and approached a house. A man and a woman in the house had time to fetch a pair of binoculars and have a good look at him standing broadside a measured 53 yards away before carrying on across a field and into the woods. He was in sight at least five minutes. They described him as "two or three times the size of a bobcat," very "chunky" in build, a solid dead-grass colour with a darker tail.

A month later a panther was seen by a number of people on the outskirts of Devon, the Fredericton suburb on the northeast side of the river. It too was watched through binoculars at seventy-five yards in broad daylight, but as it was described as black, it was apparently not the same animal. Police were called and reassuring announcements made to avoid panic. It disappeared with no unfortunate incidents.

Then on November 26, 1963, a panther was seen at the northern edge of the range by two deer hunters. It was digging in a field and they thought it must be after field mice. They both fired at it, but it was too far away and they missed. It took cover at once, in dense spruce, and they found an eight- to ten-inch hole where it had been digging.

It was just getting dark, and they walked up to the edge of the spruce. Here they found two hauling roads on either side of the place where the panther had entered the woods. They stood and discussed what they had seen. Then each took a road and they started into the woods on the last of the light. They had not gone fifty yards before the panther crossed the road in front of one of the hunters "moving at tremendous speed." He fired two shots, but they did not touch it.

They agreed the body was nearer four than three feet long, and the tail another three feet. The animal was buff-coloured, with white, or near-white, on the chest and underparts, and it was a large and apparently well-fed animal. Its speed was "terrific."

It appeared again on September 1, 1964, about ten miles from where it was last seen. It stood for fifteen minutes on the edge of a main road watching a man who moved very slowly toward it. He was within fifty yards when a car came along the road. The panther turned and ran "with the curious running gait of a lion raising both forelegs together." It jumped some high bushes and disappeared, and was not seen again that year.

The following report from this region took place the day after Christmas, 1965. It was within a mile of the place where the small panther had come out of the Portobello swamps and tried to cross the St. John River at Maugerville in 1948.

By 6 p.m. on December 26 the night was dark, snowing and blowing hard. A panther following the moose and deer crossing from the head of the Portobello to the river sat watching the headlights of cars passing on the main Trans-Canada Highway. Waiting its chance, it darted across the road unseen. Between it and the river now lay only a tussock marsh and a few small houses along the bank.

When it was halfway across the tussock marsh a car turned off the highway onto the road running down to the houses on the bank. About 100 yards short of them the car got stuck in the snow of this unploughed road. At this point the panther was standing in the tussock marsh watching. It walked over curiously and stepped onto the road in the headlights just as a woman left the house behind it and started to walk to the car.

At once a great shouting began in the car, but it was blowing so hard she could not hear what the occupants were trying to tell her. They were shouting to her to go back. Mrs. Thelma Cody said: "When I first saw the animal it was in the headlights which were shining right at me. It was sort of crouched over, and I thought it was a bear."

It moved off the road and two of the occupants of the car went to her and brought her to it.

"When we got to the car it was only about thirty feet away, broadside on, and I saw it was a huge cat."

The panther moved off into the tussock marsh and stood watching them, until one man produced a shotgun from the car and fired at it. Even then it only moved farther away, and a boy had time to run back to the house, get a second shotgun, and take another shot at it before it vanished in the darkness. Even after the second shot it moved off slowly and at ease, so it was obviously not hit.

Three days later Mrs. Cody was still nervous when talking about her experience. She had suffered the usual fate of people who have reported seeing a panther, and she was told that what she had seen was a fox or a police dog.

"Last summer several of the children came home with what we thought was a wild tale," Mrs. Cody added. "They said they saw a huge cat sleeping out in the marsh. No one paid any attention to them, but they took me back and pointed out where they had seen it. There was nothing there, but I noted that an ordinary cat could not have been seen from where they stood, if lying down, because the grass was too high.

"Now no one believes the six of us who saw and fired twice at such an animal from thirty-forty feet away. It was a huge cat."

On July 4, 1966, two men were walking in to their pulp camp on the Acadia Forest Experiment Station in Sunbury County. It was 9:30 p.m. and the light was fading fast. A panther crossed the road several hundred feet ahead of them, and stood on the side of the road watching as they came up. They were only separated from it by half the width of the road and the ditch. It did not snarl or growl but stood and looked at them.

They picked up stones and threw them at it, attempting to pass. But it turned and walked along the edge of the bushes parallel to them for about 300 feet. When a stone landed particularly close it turned toward them, and they did not try to hit it. Finally it disappeared into the gloom of the forest. That night something frightened their horse so badly that it broke the door off the hovel and got out, but it was not injured.

They described the animal as four feet long with a three-foot tail, and reddish-brown in colour.

That same evening I was hidden in the bushes beside the road playing a recording of the calls of a female mountain lion in heat through a loudspeaker to the silent forest. An owl had been hooting at dusk, but stopped as soon as I turned on the recording. At the last of the light I clearly saw a dark shape step out on to the road. It took three steps directly toward me and then turned back into the bush. It was at the limit of visibility.

The animal was long, low and heavy, and it was definitely not a deer. I cannot say it was a panther because I could not see it clearly enough, but I believe it was. Its movements were certainly feline, and it was too large for a lynx or a bobcat.

Between 1904-70, panthers were trapped and shot, wounded and escaped, or just seen by people who took the trouble to report them a total of fifty-eight times in this region. Two of these were females with cubs, and four were reported to be black. They caused panic at one country school, and the Fredericton City Police were alerted to their presence on at least two occasions. One calf received non-fatal injuries.

The Juniper Range

To the north and east of the Central Range the country changes from the long, level-topped ridges, covered with mixed-wood forests many times cut over, to irregular, higher and more broken hills. The mixed-wood forest changes rather suddenly to a preponderance of spruce and fir in the valleys between hardwood ridges, as the edge of the great spruce-fir forests of northern New Brunswick is reached. This latter is known as the "greenwoods" to the local guides and woodsmen.

The centre of these spruce-fir forests holds very little food for deer. The closed canopy has nothing beneath it, within the reach of a deer, but dead branches and moss. For this reason, deer are more strictly edge animals in this region, and it is along the fringes of these dark and dismal forests that the panthers hunt.

In September 1939, a panther lay on a rock ledge on the western face of a tall hill, overlooking the valley of the North Branch of the Southwest Miramichi River. It lay all morning, lazing in the warm sun, but about noon it became restless.

The heavy tail swung from side to side as it balanced the

animal during the steep descent of the hill. The panther approached the river in the valley below. The big cat was not particularly hungry, but when its keen ears picked up the scratching of a family of partridges ahead it could not resist a stalk. Silently it slid forward until it was ten yards from the unsuspecting birds. They were in the trail used by the river drivers in the spring that runs along the whole length of the river.

The panther lay watching the partridges as they searched among the dead leaves, until it lost interest and stood up. Still the birds did not see it behind a screen of bushes. The panther's interest was focused on the trail behind the partridges. There stood a man with a rifle in his hands, staring at the panther. Raymond Sweet raised the rifle and aimed, then quietly lowered it again. In a flash the panther had cleared a windfall and was gone. The rifle rang out behind.

"Partly concealed by small trees was what I thought to be a small deer. Raising my rifle I took aim and was about to shoot when I decided I did not want a deer as early as this, so I lowered the rifle. At that moment the animal bounded into a small clearing and over an old windfall giving me an excellent view. I took a quick shot and missed."

Seven years later a full-grown panther wandered to the west into the settled country. It spent the late summer and fall on the hardwood ridges above the fields, and prowling along the alder-lined brooks that thread the valleys. It was lying on a log across one of these brooks one day, enjoying the warmth of a bright sun, and was nearly asleep. It had lain for some time on the log when a sound aroused it. Looking up it stared straight into the face of a man standing about twenty yards away. He had approached along the brook where the noise of his coming was muffled by the running water, and the surprise was mutual. The man seemed to have hardly time to blink before the log was deserted, leaving him rubbing his unbelieving eyes. He could hardly credit what he had seen. For a long time afterwards he mentioned it to nobody as he was afraid of ridicule. Then after others had come forward to tell of seeing a panther, he told of his own experience.

One day in September 1946, a panther fell asleep stretched full length on warm sand. Some time later a crunching noise brought it fully awake. The animal lifted its head and stared down the long ribbon of sand until it was lost around a corner of the hill. Nothing was in sight. Puzzled, the panther swung its head slowly to look behind. Within a few feet stood a man astride a bicycle staring at it open-mouthed. The long strip of hard earth and sand where it had lain down to drowse in the sun was a road. The man had seen the animal from a distance but could not make out what it was. He had bicycled up quietly to within a few feet before he realized the animal stretched out on the road in front of him was a full-grown panther. It reached the woods in one bound, and he reached the next house in record time. The place was only three miles from where the panther had been surprised on the log two months before.

The following spring it was back on Beadle Brook in the deep forest to the east, far from the settlements. Here it occupied the range about the mountain between the upper Beadle Brook and the North Branch of the Southwest Miramichi.

As the sun went down behind the high hills, still white-topped in late April, the panther left the high ground where it had lain up and descended to the old bulldozed road. It had been made eight years before, but the traffic was so light that it was already full of dead grass. The road was a favourite place for deer to get into the open when the melting snow released them from their winter yards each spring, and the panther made full use of it in his hunts.

That evening it was just starting to get dark as the animal reached the road. It stepped out on the path and gave a long searching stare as far as it could see. There was nothing in sight, and as it swung its head, a movement behind it caught its eye. A man with an axe in one hand and fumbling with a holstered pistol with the other stood staring at the animal. In one bound the panther was in deep cover. Drawing his pistol the man ran to where it had disappeared, but there was nothing. The muskrat trapper of Beadle Brook went all the way back to his lonely cabin below the dead water with a loaded pistol in his hand that night.

One of the females the panther visited lived well to the north. Waugh Ridge, the divide between the watershed of the North Branch of the Southwest Miramichi and the Rivière de Chute, was the border of her home territory where she usually met her big mate when he ranged up from the rugged hills to the south. In October 1947, she had come into heat and she searched out all his old scent posts and deposited her scent. At night she prowled the ridge calling.

On the third day she had received no answer to her calls, and found no fresh sign anywhere on the ridge. Her unrequited ardour was at its peak, and she prowled restlessly from one end of the long ridge to the other. Below her lay a dense black spruce swamp that the big male would have to cross when he came. She watched it anxiously, and on this day her keen eyes picked up the swaying of the small dense trees as a large animal forced its way through.

Instantly she was all alert, and, watching keenly, she was able to predict where the animal crossing the swamp would come out on the dry ground at the foot of the ridge. When it got there she was only sixty feet away.

But this was not her long awaited mate. Instead, two very tired and dirty deer hunters stumbled out of the swamp and settled gratefully on a log to rest. They sat and talked in low voices for about twenty minutes, and then rose and started up the old tote road to the ridge. As they stood up Gordon Tweedie looked straight into the eyes of the female panther standing on the trunk of a fallen tree, about five feet above the ground.

"It was very curious and very much interested in us but showed no ferocity whatever. I waved my arm to see what it would do and it very quickly turned tail toward us, but still stood and looked back over its shoulder for a few seconds and it was at this point when I decided to shoot.

"As I threw my rifle up it hopped off the log on the opposite side and that was the last we saw of it. . . . The thing that impressed me most was the long tail which I estimated would be twenty-four to twenty-eight inches long, and the last four inches . . . seemed to be turned up sharply. Another thing that impressed me was the tremendous size of the forelegs, as they seemed to me to be larger than my own wrists."

The hunters spent the night in a little camp only 200 yards away, and just after dark the female called once. Instead of her longed-for mate, her most deadly enemies had come to her territory. She did not call again during their stay.

When spring came to the Juniper country the following year, 1948, the sleek silver salmon climbed the many-branched Miramichi, as the grouse boomed on their drumming logs and the muskrats began their breeding season in the deadwaters. The deer shed their winter coat of dull grey for the rusty new hair of summer, and the great gaunt moose moved thankfully to the swamps for the first of the new green pondweeds.

The woodcock buzzed in the clearings morning and night as the paired black ducks sought out the remote beaver ponds to nest. Spring turned to summer and the young of the year were everywhere, but there was no sign of the panthers. Deep in the trackless forest to the northeast the female had given birth to a litter of cubs. For a time she would not tolerate her mate, and he wandered away by himself.

When summer was drawing to a close he reached the Alder-grounds near Juniper, and made his presence known to man. He was in that dangerously complacent mood of tolerating men, when he would not hide at once, but would stay and watch them in plain sight. He was safe as long as he played this game only with unarmed men, but the season of the guns was approaching and men were trying them out.

Three times in twenty-four hours he deliberately let men approach within thirty yards, before he moved off. The last time he watched a man fishing from a bridge for some time. The man seemed harmless enough, and the panther stepped out on the road and stood looking at him from thirty yards away. The man froze and made no effort to move, and the panther walked on up the road for about 100 yards before stepping off into the woods. After this his curiosity seemed satisfied and he left the neighbourhood of the settlement.

By late March 1949, a panther was not far from the Forks of the Upper Miramichi River, and in the territory of a noted guide and trapper who had been trying to trap it for a long time. It rounded a bend in the trail to find a thick spruce had fallen across it.

At first glance it looked as if it would have to climb through the heavy branches over the log, and being full and lazy it did not relish the thought of this. It walked up to the blow-down and stood looking the obstacle over. At once it noticed that there was a way underneath. A convenient passage had been cleared through the branches under the log which was just large enough for it to squeeze through. As it forced its heavy shoulders through the narrow opening it hardly felt the loop of strong wire that slid over its head and around its powerful neck.

It felt the closing noose begin to tighten, but it thought it nothing more than another branch that it would push aside with its chest. As its head emerged on the far side it lunged ahead to break clear — and hit the end of the wire. The noose jerked it over on its back, but it tore at the wire with its claws. Relentlessly the noose drew tighter, and it was held firmly tight by a patent lock that did not allow it to slack off. All that saved the panther were its mighty neck muscles, as the noose had closed just in front of its shoulders. It could still breathe, but only just. Then the struggle began.

Had the snare been made fast to a light drag log that the panther could have moved it would have been doomed, but instead the trapper had secured it to the main trunk of the felled tree. This gave the great cat something solid to pull against. All through the long night it rolled and twisted and fought the strangling wire. By dawn it was still at it and there was a great red welt around its neck where the wire had bitten through hair and hide to raw flesh.

For the hundredth time the panther lunged to the end of the wire with all its strength from where it had been lying resting alongside the log. It had learned that it could breathe more easily when there was no tension on the wire, and it took its moments of rest against the log. This time the one in a million chance that could save it took place. The wire kinked a second before the weight came on it, and broke with a singing snap as the animal's full weight, backed by every ounce of its furious strength, came against it. The panther was free — almost.

It lay for a minute not realizing it was no longer tethered, for the wire around its neck, now completely buried in a puffy ring of raw flesh, was still strangling it, and its breathing came in hoarse gasps. Even with the snap of the wire the patent lock held. It could just breathe, but it could never eat again. It stumbled off toward the river.

Later that day the trapper, Fred Grant, visited his set. He stood and marvelled at the torn-up wreckage of his elaborate snare set, and he examined the tracks in the snow. He looked at the end of the snapped wire, and a low whistle of amazement escaped him.

"Eight-ply 20-gauge wire! And he broke it!"

He followed the track to the river and then to where it turned to the mountain. There he gave up and went home.

Nothing more was ever heard of the big panther. It starved, slowly strangling from the wire embedded in its neck, in the silent forests of the upper Miramichi.

A month later, on December 3, 1956, Mr. and Mrs. Fred Grant of Juniper were able to sketch a three-quarter-grown panther from life at the range of fifty feet. They were travelling by jeep along a woods road leading to the headwaters of the Nashwaak River. The panther was standing in the road facing them, about 100 yards away when first seen. They drove up to within fifty feet and stopped. They had no camera, but they did have their lunch and a pencil. Unwrapping the lunch, Fred Grant made the sketch on the wrapping paper.

The animal was a young one, not much bigger than a big bobcat. It stood an estimated twenty-six inches at the shoulders, with a body length of thirty-six inches and a tail of equal length. It was a very light brown on the back and sides, with no spots, and creamy white underneath. It had clearly marked eye-stripes on the forehead, and black patches on each side of the upper lip. The ears were tipped with black and the head seemed small for the size of the body. It showed no fear of the jeep, and stayed in sight long enough for the sketch to be completed before bounding away.

This youngster had just lost its spots, but it may not have left its mother. She may have been lying nearby unnoticed, watching her brash cub standing for its portrait. The incident took place in the deep woods, about thirty miles from where the mating calls had been heard the previous summer, and the animal had the whole of the central forests of New Brunswick to roam in without contacting man. This it did, and nothing more was heard of panthers in this region for three years.


The Northwest Range

This is "The Republic of Madawaska," long known for its light regard for laws originating in the provincial capital of Fredericton. I had long wondered why I received no panther reports from this region, as it is just as good deer range as the areas on all sides that were reporting panthers.

I attributed this lack to the fact that the local people were French-speaking and that there was a language barrier. Then one day I received a letter from an employee of the local pulp company which contained an eye-opening sentence. He reported a panther on the Green River Road and ended his letter with a plea that I tell no one he had written to me "because I can lose my job."

It never occurred to me that wildlife reports could be considered classified information by some companies. This perhaps explains why letters of inquiry I had addressed to a woods manager of a pulp company in southeastern Quebec regarding some panther information I had received from his limits went unanswered.

This is still the only report I have received from this region, and it is about five years old. I do not believe panthers are any scarcer here than elsewhere in northern New Brunswick, but reports certainly are.


The Restigouche — Nepisiguit Range

The north coast of New Brunswick is drained by two main rivers and a number of smaller ones. The first in importance of the main rivers is the world-famous Restigouche where the largest salmon south of the St. Lawrence run to spawn. Here are some of the most valuable sport fishing rights in the world, leased to private clubs and jealously guarded.

The other main river is the Nepisiguit, which also has a run of salmon, but is not comparable to the Restigouche. The watersheds of both these rivers and the smaller ones between are the limits of large pulp and paper companies and are being cut over continuously. The forest is, therefore, in a series of different age blocks, is well broken up, and parts of it are good deer country. Along with the deer come the long-tailed cats.

On November 9, 1948, a pair of panthers were hunting along the edges of Levesque's Bog on the Southeast Upsalquitch, a tributary of the Restigouche coming in from the south. They had spent all their lives in the great central forest and had never experienced any harm from the distant gunfire they had occasionally heard. To them it was just another loud noise. When they came to the bog they separated and one went along each side to intercept any deer which jumped in the centre.

The male stepped out of cover and stood looking over the open area ahead. He swung his head slowly around until he was looking at the hillside to his left where a movement caught his eye. He could make nothing of it and stood staring quietly as a rifle rang out from the hill and the bullet snapped into the

57

Labrador Tea beside him. Never having associated the sound of a rifle, which he had heard a few times before in the distance, with danger, he paid it no attention and turned and walked away, searching over the bog.

A man's voice rang out from a dense clump of black spruce asking what his partner was shooting at. The rifle rang out again and the female on the other side of the bog leaped six feet in the air as something snapped across under her belly. When the excited deer hunters burst from cover to look for signs of a hit, both panthers lost no time in getting under cover. They watched curiously for a few moments and then faded into the forest. They would find another bog which was not so crowded.

They withdrew into the hills that are drained by the Southeast Upsalquitch, the Tetagouche, and the Forty-Four Mile Brook of the Nepisiguit. Here the female selected her den and gave birth to a litter of cubs. Among them was one of an odd grey and black pattern that was quite different from the others. Their mother hunted for them along the edges of the great highland barrens of this region as they grew up. It was on these same barrens that the caribou had ranged in numbers not so long before, but now deer and moose around the edge were all there was left.

By the spring of 1951 the litter had broken up and the cubs were on their own. The odd-coloured one had wandered down Forty-Four Mile Brook to the Nepisiguit River where it found many rabbits and grouse to support it while it perfected its deer-killing technique. Its tracks were frequently seen along the company road, and some of the truck drivers caught a glimpse of it as it darted into cover to let the roaring monsters pass. Word got around that there was a panther cub in the valley.

By fall it had reached full size, and the grey and black cub had become jet black all over. On September 17, 1951, it stood on the company road just sixteen miles from Bathurst in a pouring rain. A car rounded a bend only seventy feet away and the driver saw "a young bear" standing before him. As the "young bear" turned to leave he saw the long tail and realized he was looking at that great rarity, a black panther in North America.

Two summers later one of the family was spending the hot weather along the well-shaded banks of the Southeast Upsal-quitch where the salmon lay in the pools and the fishermen spent endless hours casting over them. At the famous Two-Mile Pool, four guides and wardens sat on the bank waiting for their fishermen who were coming along behind. The sound of the swiftly moving water drowned out their soft talk.

Suddenly a guide looked up, gestured for silence, and pointed across the river. A full-grown panther stepped out of the bushes on the far bank and walked along the beach to the end of the bar, less than 100 yards away. In the bright sun it seemed a little lighter in colour than a deer. It stood giving them a perfect view of its long heavy tail. It was larger than a Great Dane dog, but longer and heavier in the forequarters. When the fishermen arrived the panther had gone back into the forest, and the excited guides told them what they had missed.

During the deer season of 1957, a big male was on the hills about Nepisiguit Lake. There is much burned and cutover country here, and some of it is covered with long grass. He stood watching as a deer hunter worked over the slope of the next hill. His only movement was a slight wave of the tip of the heavy tail as he watched the hunter, who had not seen him, sit down about 150 yards away, raise his rifle, and start glassing the slope through the 'scope.

He stood broadside to the man, with a stump covering his mid-section, and as the swing of the rifle came closer and closer he froze and stood motionless. The glass crossed the stump, stopped, and came back and settled firmly on him. He did not move until finally the man lowered his rifle to rest his aching arms. Then he slunk quietly away. When the rifle came up again, still and steady and ready to fire, there was nothing to be seen.

The hunter walked back and forth for ten minutes, glassing the slope, before he found the panther sitting on the top of the hill watching him from between some stumps. Very carefully, and not taking his eyes off the animal, he walked backward about fifteen yards to a level spot and lay down. Only the head and chest of the cat were above the dead grass but he was shooting a .270 rifle with a 4 power 'scope at 175 yards. Normally he could hit a dollar bill regularly at this distance.

He put the cross hairs squarely in the centre of the panther's chest and squeezed off the shot. The cat went over backwards and disappeared at once. The hunter rose and ran down the hill only to find a deep brook that he could not cross at the bottom. He had to make a detour which took him into a swamp. By the time he got out it was dark, so he returned to camp.

After supper he and three guides set out with an axe and a lantern to bring in the panther. It was a beautiful moonlit night and they reached the spot with no difficulty. They found an overturned stump where the cat had whirled at the shot - but no panther.

The next morning the hunter checked his rifle and found the sight was out of line, "and I must have missed the panther by about thirty feet."

In 1959 the black specimen was seen again on the International Paper Company Road, only six miles south of Dalhousie. It crossed the road at high noon in front of a jeep carrying three members of a Mines Department survey party. It moved slowly and in no hurry across in front of them, and gave them a good opportunity to observe it carefully. At this time it was about nine years old and was full-grown.

The survey party had been working in the Ramsay Brook area all summer. They had found the remains of about twenty dead deer which were not winter kills, so at least one panther had probably been in the area for some time. It is unusual for a male to stay for any length of time in one area, and so this was probably the territory of a female. The number of kills in a relatively small area suggests she may have reared a litter of cubs there. This was suspected but not proved until the following summer, when on July 10, 1960, two members of the New Brunswick Forest Service passed a half-grown cub on the side of the road along the main Upsalquitch River. It was normally coloured and was "definitely a cougar." They passed it within twenty-five yards.

The next summer a fisherman was working his way up the Northwest Upsalquitch when he noticed freshly disturbed gravel on a bar ahead. Some stones had been overturned so recently that they had not had time to dry. He saw marks of a furious struggle on the bar, and at the shoreward edge under the alders lay the carcass of a deer. It was a doe and its head was torn off and one hind leg eaten. It was a hot day, but the flies had not yet found it so the kill was very fresh.

The fisherman was not thinking about panthers in this region, and he concluded the doe must have been killed by a bear. He was uneasy, and unarmed, so he left without further examining the deer.

There was an excellent berry crop in the district at the time, and black bears do not hunt deer in August, so it is much more probable that this was a panther's kill and the fisherman's approach had frightened off the cat. Two panther sight records were made within a mile of the spot.

This is the last we have heard to date of writing of the panthers of the Restigouche-Nepisiguit region. They still haunt the beautiful rivers and high rocky hills. As mechanization of logging brings more machines but much fewer men into the woods, it seems probable that the animals will continue to survive at their present low level. With the whole of their range in managed pulpwood limits, annual cuts of large size that will set back the forest succession and maintain a large deer population are assured. The panther's natural caution has kept it away from hunters on all but one occasion so far, and, if no new devices are introduced, this may be expected to continue. The future of the several families of big cats along the northern rim of the province seems secure at this writing.


The Miramichi Range

In this clockwise swing through the panther country of New Brunswick, the next region to be considered is that great watershed drained by many rivers and brooks that finally come together in the stream the Indians called "The Little Goodly River." It is known by another Indian name today—the Miramichi. This river rises in the central highlands of northern New Brunswick, and stretches all the way from the Juniper country in the west over 100 miles to the Bartibogue in the east.

It was on the upper reaches of these rivers that what became one of the most significant events in the history of New Brunswick began. It was October 1825, after a dry summer, and the leaf-carpeted forest was tinder dry. Then it started. A curl of smoke here. Another ten miles away in the next valley. Lightning, or man? It did not matter. Soon the sky was full of smoke in all directions, and fires dotted the horizon. As modern foresters would say, the fire hazard was extreme and had been so for many days.

As the fires grew they created their own wind. Soon a hurricane was blowing and the conditions of a "firestorm," such as first studied after massed bombings in World War II, were created. It burned parts of central New Brunswick to bare gravel, and it wiped out the towns of Newcastle and Douglastown. At least 160 people died.

It was from this fire that the wildlife history of the region dates today.

Seventy-five years after the Miramichi Fire, the barrens created by the burn was well-covered with caribou moss, and herds of woodland caribou roamed the interior. Moose and deer were found in the lowlands along the rivers that had been too wet to burn.

A female panther had given birth to her cubs in a den amid a pile of rocks on a wooded hillside overlooking the game trail leading from the interior barrens to the river. This trail was often used by the caribou crossing the river, and they provided her with kills within a few hundred yards of her den.

This day she had not been on her lookout long when the clicking of hooves warned her of the approach of caribou. An old doe led the group as it passed in single file below, followed by a magnificent stag. Bringing up the rear was a yearling.

Not a muscle of the beautiful bundle of sinews that lay flat on the rock as the caribou passed quivered until the last reached the point under her. Then a brown blur flashed from the rock in a twenty-foot leap and landed squarely on the yearling. The shock of 100 pounds of bone and muscle travelling at full speed knocked it flat, but it never left the embrace of those steely forearms. The long teeth met in its vertebrae, and it died without a sound. The rest of the group proceeded to cross the river and disappear from the panther's world.

A half-mile downstream two men stood in a heavily loaded canoe and laboured steadily at poling it against the fast current. One was to become a Professor of Natural Science at the University of New Brunswick, and the other was an Indian guide. A third man walked along the bank to lighten the load. He was a keen naturalist, and experienced hunter and a good observer.

The panther lay on her kill for a few moments to be sure it was dead. Then she licked off what blood there was on both the kill and herself, rose, and, grasping the yearling by the back of the neck, she began to pull it back up the hill to the den. She had not gone far when she heard something approaching. Dropping the caribou she retreated instinctively toward the den and took cover. The first man she had ever seen stepped onto the trail and stood staring at the caribou.

Dr. William J. Long examined the carcass, noting that nothing had been eaten and that it had not been covered. It was obviously fresh. He realized that he had frightened off the killer—a bear or a panther. Cautiously he followed another twenty or thirty yards in the direction of the drag, eyes alert for any movement. When he got to within twenty yards of the panther, crouched unseen beside the trail, her nerve broke and she turned and ran. He caught a flash of a dun-coloured animal, and knew the killer was not a bear.

Turning, he ran back down the hill and waved in the oncoming canoe. Seizing his rifle he returned to the kill and with the safety off and finger on the trigger, he followed in the direction of the drag.

"When the canoe came in sight I waved it ashore and hurried back, rifle in hand, to where I had glimpsed the killer. Following his direction I came (within 100 yards or so) to a great hollow in the wooded hillside. The upper part was a jumble of bare rocks; the lower part, free of underbrush, was partly moss-covered, partly patches of bare earth. On the upper side was a big hole among the rocks. In front of the hole the earth was trodden, telling of a den.

"After waiting a while—not very long because the canoe was working up-river, and might pass, and be hard for me to find again—I crawled into the hole pushing the rifle ahead of me. The hole opened into a pocket, dark as pitch, filled with a nauseating odor of cat and carrion. After waiting at the entrance a minute or two, I scratched a match, which gave light enough for me to see that the den was empty. Then I backed out. Searching around the hollow I found a few pug marks, one bigger than any footprint of a bobcat or Canada lynx that I had ever seen; the others small by comparison.

"I think, therefore, that I had stumbled upon the kill and the den of a panther, that she had at least one kit, that she sensed my coming and stole away before I crawled into the den."

Eight years later, in the fall of 1908, is the first definite report of crippling loss among New Brunswick panthers. At that time two men set out on a caribou hunt up Porter Brook, a stream that joins the Miramichi a few miles above Boiestown. The teamster and the cook were half a mile ahead of the two hunters when the last man thought he saw a deer leap from some tall grass that bordered an alder swale.

Both hunters turned back to investigate, and a persistent feeling came over the one that had seen the movement that it was not a deer. They had not gone far when they found what they were looking for. Along the limb of a tree twenty feet from the ground, and only about thirty feet from him, the leader saw a full-grown panther. As soon as it realized it had been seen, it bared its teeth and lashed its long heavy tail.

The hunter aimed his .30-.30 Winchester at the front shoulder and fired. The cat dropped from the branch, hung momentarily by its hind paws, and then fell with a thud into the tall grass and alders at the foot of the tree. Here it was out of sight—and they never saw it again. J. W. Fairley said: "McKiel and I hunted for days for that cat and never did find him. . . . That cat had a tail a good three feet long and I would judge the body to be about twice as long as the tail. Incidently, that tail kept lashing all the time the cat was looking at me; no other movement."

A dog was all that was needed to follow up and end the suffering of that dying cat, but caribou hunters do not use dogs. A great panther died that day, drowning in its own blood as its perforated lungs filled; an animal so rare that even the mention of its name draws ridicule, its one sin that it had been seen by a man with the power to kill it. No one ever found the body. It was the first panther killed by white men in New Brunswick of which there is a record.

The panther family from north of the Miramichi moved east that winter and wandered out to the edge of the settlement. A routine report from Forest Ranger Perley W. Vanderbeck states that one was seen on the Red Bank to Quarryville road, and two were trapped six miles to the east. There is no other record of these specimens. Three panthers travelling together could only be a female with two well-grown cubs, and, as we will see, such groups have more than once blundered into towns and even the outskirts of Canada's largest city.

In November 1923, an event occurred on the headwaters of the Sevogle River which has only been duplicated twice since. The only record of what took place is the following story, that appeared on page one of the Saint John *Telegraph Journal* on November 24, 1923.

"SHOOTS A PANTHER IN NEW BRUNSWICK. ANIMAL RARELY FOUND IN THE PROVINCE KILLED IN NORTHUMBERLAND.

"Newcastle, November 22: While superintending the work in the lumber woods on the headwaters of the Sevogle River last week, Collingwood Fraser, foreman for William M. Sullivan Ltd., saw a large animal which he thought was a wildcat. Procuring a rifle, Mr. Fraser fired and wounded the animal, whereupon it charged him, but a second shot fired when the beast was less than five feet away killed the animal, which upon examination proved to be a panther or cougar.

"Persons who saw it say it measured about four feet in length and had a tail almost as long as its body.

"The cougar is very rarely found in this province and how this one made its way into the heart of New Brunswick's forests is considered considerable of a mystery."

It certainly is not strange than any large carnivore would attempt to defend itself when wounded, and there is no mystery about how it happened to be on the headwaters of the Sevogle River. It was born there.

Thus it appears that four panthers were killed by man in this sector between 1908 and 1923. The first was mortally wounded and lost, the next two were trapped, and the last one was shot. Is there any connection between this fact and the emergence of one of the most persistent folk legends of the New Brunswick forests —the Dungarvon Whooper?

The Dungarvon is a river, a tributary of the Miramichi joining the Renous just before it runs into the main stream. It runs from west to east, draining a watershed between that of the Bartholomew and the South Renous, and is a famous lumbering area. Just about this time a story came out of the Dungarvon country about how men in the camps at night had heard wild and frightening screams coming from the jet black frozen forest of a winter night. The Whooper terrified grown men who had spent their lives in the lumber woods.

The screams were heard at long intervals over a period of several years, and then they ceased. However, a legend was born and has been rolling ever since. Tales of a lunatic loose in the woods were bandied about, and the timid refused to be left alone at night. It was even suggested that it might have been a panther, but the more alarming suggestions were more acceptable. However, a female panther coming into heat and seeking a mate in a range where the adult male had been killed and had not been replaced would give her wild screams at intervals until she was requited or her period had passed. Was one of the four panthers killed her mate? And were the only survivors left to replace him her own cubs? Were her wild and lonely screams, echoing through the dark forests of the Dungarvon, evidence that she had been left unattended for yet another year? It seems likely.

In the summer of 1931, four fishermen sat on the verandah of the camp at the Square Forks of the Sevogle River, about two hours before dark, waiting for the evening meal. About 150 yards away an animal appeared swimming across to the south bank. When it reached the shore it stopped, giving them plenty of time to observe it. Dr. Arthur S. Chesley described it.

"He was a cat measuring from rump to snout about five or six feet. His face was long (not flat or chopped off like a wildcat). His fur was long and light in colour. I do not recall any striping or spots. He impressed me as being similar to a Jaguar or Leopard. We called the three guides. . . . Machette brought a rifle, took aim and fired. The bullet lit just above his nose and with one graceful leap this animal landed on top of this ten- or twelve-foot rock and ran into the woods."

There are now to be considered a group of records that must be separated from those north of the river. They come from the vicinity of Black River and Napan on the south shore of Miramichi Bay.

In the fall of 1947 two men were walking along a trail at the head of Robichaud Brook below Loggieville. They were hunting and the man ahead carried a .22 pistol for partridges and snowshoe hares. The man behind carried a rifle. As they rounded a bend they met a panther in the trail coming toward them. It stopped instantly and stared.

"My God Uncle Jim, look! A cougar! Give me the rifle."

He turned to get it and the panther was off in a flash back the way it had come in twenty-foot bounds. Its nearest approach was just twenty-six feet from where he stood. He never got off a shot.

In the fall of 1948 tracks were reported by the game warden in this area, and several people, including the warden, saw a strange animal that they could not identify. He reported cautiously to his head office on December 18, 1948 that he had seen an animal he could not identify, but that it looked like a panther.

The last report of this family was on February 25, 1957, nine years after the first tracks were seen in the area. A man and his wife, R.C.A.F. personnel from a nearby air base, watched a "cougar or mountain lion" run across a field from their kitchen window.

A pair was reported on Parker Ridge during the summer of 1963. This is just across the river from Porter Brook where the first New Brunswick panther was shot and lost in 1908. On October 12, 1968, two bird hunters on the Dungarvon Road also saw a panther.

Thus we know that the thin tenuous thread of the scattered families of this region has survived, and they are probably as numerous today as they have ever been.


The Kent-Westmorland Range

This sector includes the country south of the Kent-Northumberland line to the Nova Scotia border. It is generally flat for the most part, with a thick second growth of mixed wood forest. The western part is a large forest containing few settlements and the Canaan Game Refuge. Along the east coast are some of the oldest Acadian settlements in New Brunswick. In the southeast, the region joins the heavily wooded hills of Cumberland County, Nova Scotia, which support one of the best deer and moose population in that province.

Panther activity in this region has been relatively slight. The first reference to the species is the use of the name Catamount for a small settlement northeast of Moncton. In 1882 the settlement road is recorded at the Deeds Office in Fredericton as the Reserve Road. In 1891 the same road is called the Catamount Road, and no explanation for the change can be found. In those ten years something happened in this area to give the name of

*The eye-stripe of the panther is an indication of age. The specimen above is immature; the one below is an adult. Photo: Bruce S. Wright.*

*The photos at the top left and right are of scrapes in the snow—clear evidence that an eastern panther has recently passed that way. The summer photo in the middle, also shows a panther's scrape, with the print of a hind paw in the depression. (Photos Bruce S. Wright).*

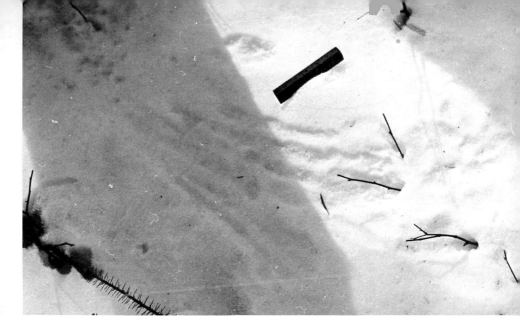

*Bottom left: The cased skin of the first New Brunswick panther ever photographed is held aloft by a hunter in 1932. (Photo Roy Grant) Bottom right: The carcass of a specimen shot in Pennsylvania in 1967. (Photo Pittsburgh Press).*

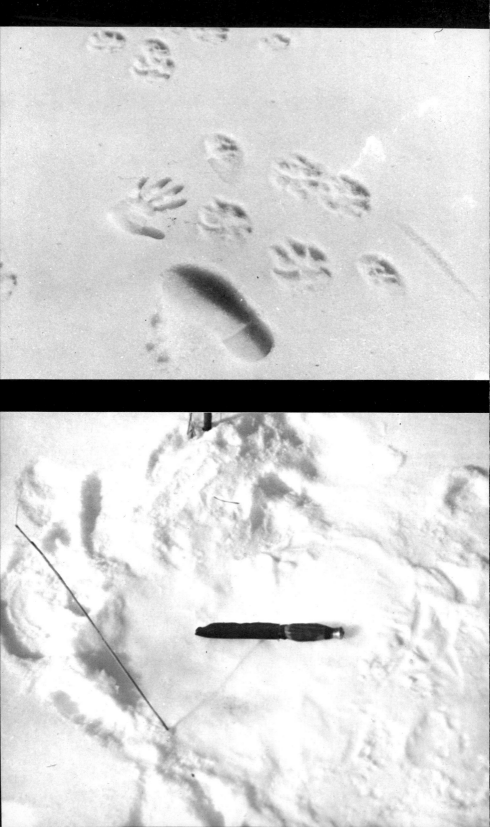

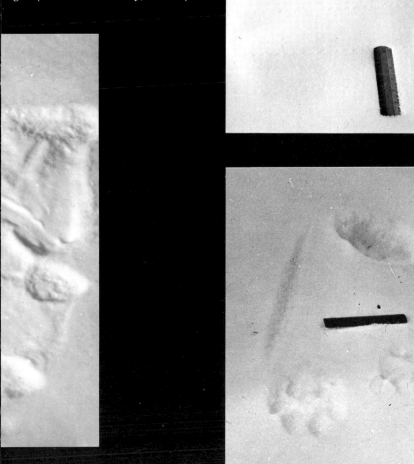

*Top left: The first evidence of breeding in New Brunswick—tracks of a female and her cub going from right to left, those of a male going from left to right. The author's hand- and foot-print give the scale. (Photo Bruce S. Wright)*

*Right top and bottom: The trail of an old male in the Fundy Hills of New Brunswick. Note the splaying of the toes. (Photos Bruce S. Wright) Bottom left: The bed of a small panther. Note the mark of the long tail beginning at the left and stretching across the bottom to the lower right. (Photo Lt. Devaney, R.H.C.)*

*The northern race of the eastern panther which has never been photographed alive. The Little St. John Lake Specimen. Photo Northeastern Wildlife Station.*

*A panther silhouetted against the light, as above, will appear black, whereas in fact it may be dark brown, reddish or greyish, which is more common. Photos Wilfred L. Miller.*

*Above: Plaster casts of panther tracks in snow, from Ontario on the left, and in soft earth, from New Brunswick, on the right. (Photo Northeastern Wildlife Station)*
*Below: The drag-mark made by a panther's tail shows up clearly in the snow. (Photo Bruce S. Wright)*

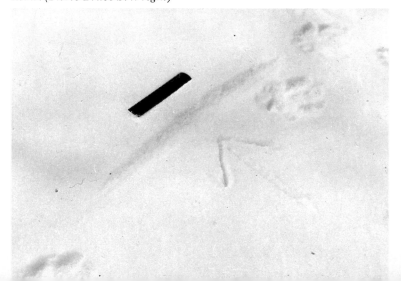

Catamount to both the road and the settlement. So far I have been unable to learn what it was.

In October 1919, on the extreme northern edge of the region south of Cains River between Salmon Brook and Sabbies River, a land surveyor was sitting on a log of a cutover hemlock ridge, smoking. He had a rifle across his knees. A panther climbed the ridge and approached to within thirty yards, where it apparently smelled his smoke. It then turned and went back down the hill without seeing him. He held the rifle on it when it was coming toward him but did not fire when it turned away.

The next record is of particular significance as it resulted in the first picture ever taken of a New Brunswick panther. In March of 1932, Roy Grant of Halifax was staying with Havelock Robertson of Mundleville, Kent County. Large cat tracks were reported at the rear of Robertson's field, and he and Grant went out to investigate. Robertson carried a British .303 Lee-Enfield rifle. They found the tracks without difficulty and followed them to a large pine. Lying along a branch was a panther. Robertson brought it down dead with two shots from the rifle, and they stood staring at it with no idea what it was. The closest they could come was "a big wildcat," and so they called it.

They took their "big wildcat" home and case-skinned it the way they were accustomed to skinning a muskrat. Then they took their pictures, holding up the seven-foot, three-inch skin. Cougars are normally flat-skinned, not case-skinned, and the pictures looked odd from the beginning. Grant took them back to Halifax where they appeared as "a rare nameless animal" in the Halifax *Chronicle*. The following day they were correctly identified by the well-known bobcat hunter Bonneycastle Dale, as photographs of a "cougar or mountain lion." Then they dropped from sight.

Havelock Robertson kept the skin for many years as a rug. Finally it became full of moths and he threw it out. The next year I found him, but all that remained were the pictures. The eastern panther had been recorded on film. To date no one has taken a picture of a living specimen.

This animal had wandered into the settled area where roads are frequent, and was well to the east of the main forest. It was inevitable that it would meet men in this region. Fortunately we have the record and the photographs preserved.

Fifteen years later, in October 1947, Game Warden John Tingley reported to his ranger that he had seen a panther while patrolling near the Nova Scotia border, not far from Point de Bute. It is in this region that panthers have extended their range into Nova Scotia where they were never known before. At this time Nova Scotia had one of the highest white-tailed deer population on the continent, and this was no doubt the cause of a few of the rare cats crossing into that province.


The Southern Range

This region is the country between Grand Lake and the Bay of Fundy, from the Petitcodiac River in the east to the St. John River in the west. It is high, hilly country along the Bay shore, dipping to the settled valley of the Kennebecasis, but rising to more hills and the semi-forested Canaan Valley in the north. The northwestern part of the area is rural farming country interspersed with wooded hills, but the southern portion is a very dense tangled forest covering the steep rocky hills leading out to the Bay. The thousand-foot contour comes within a half mile of the shore in many places, and the short precipitous rivers drop down through steep canyons in some of the roughest country in New Brunswick. Here is no land for those of unsound limb or weak heart.

Winter lingers long in this high country, and when summer has begun on Grand Lake to the north, and cottagers are moving out for the season there is still two feet of snow in the dark green forest on the high ground to the south. The lush growth is due to the proximity of the fog belt along the Bay of Fundy, combined with the altitude to provide abundant moisture.

The climate of Grand Lake is the most salubrious in the province, while that of the Upper Point Wolf River rivals that of northern Restigouche County, 200 miles to the north. In these rugged hills panthers have lived since the arrival of the deer.

Ironically, the first record we have from this region tells of a panther crippled for life but lost. The outlet of Grand Lake, draining all the country to the northeast and the great marshes about the western end of the lake, is the short and tidal Jemseg River. On its banks, in October 1921, Clairmont Dykeman met a panther. He fired at it with a shotgun loaded with ball, and broke its foreleg. The panther was knocked down, but rose and fled on three legs leaving blood, hair and bone splinters behind. One of the splinters, now at the Wildlife Station, is a thick, heavy piece of a round bone that resembles the radius, so the panther was maimed for life. No attempt was made to follow it up.

Two years later, in 1923, came the first definite report of cubs in the area. Mrs. Otho H. Bishop writes: "My husband, young son and I were taking a drive on an abandoned road through dense forested country behind Coverdale, Albert County. There was a deserted farm along the road. Just before coming to this farm we saw a good-sized, tawny-coloured animal with a long round tail following the road in front of us. When it reached the clearing it left the road, and sat down facing it only about ten feet from us.

"It watched us closely as we drove by and it never moved, so we got an excellent view of it. Its head was round like a cat's, and it looked like pictures of panthers I have seen.

"On the opposite side of the road was a clump of bushes where two kittens were playing quite close to the road. Like the large animal they showed no fear of us, and resembled her but were spotted, and were about the size of a large domestic cat."

Thus we know that panthers were breeding in these hills at least as early as 1923.

The next record occurred some years later in a summer of the 1930's. It is a very significant record, not because it also describes a litter of cubs, but because it tells of a mother with cubs suddenly interrupted at close range by a small girl alone and completely at their mercy. Here is the experience of Mrs. R. J. Johnson.

"It happened in the 1930's, when I was about eleven or twelve years old.

"I was riding my bicycle, a man's model, too big for me, that I could never mount or dismount without difficulty and I was on my way to Belleisle for the mail early one afternoon of a hot summer day. I was riding through the wood and as I approached the top of the hill, I saw what I took to be three house cats rolling and playing in the centre of the road. When they saw me they stopped their play and began to spit at me. I thought this very strange behaviour for house cats and slowed down. As I got nearer, two leaped through the shrubs on the south side of the road and scrambled up a tree where they hung by their claws spitting furiously. The third one stood on the roadside, hissing like a snake.

"I stopped my bicycle and stood, still a-straddle of it while I tried to fathom this mystery. They were the size of house cats, and yet they didn't act like them. Tawny brown, with dark brown markings mottled on their backs and their furious faces.

"Suddenly a huge animal leaped down from the top of the bank into the road, and stood where it landed. It was about four feet long in the body with a tail that seemed as long as itself, covered with short hair, as was all of it, of a tawny brown colour, with darker colouring on the head which was big, and in it were two of the largest, yellow, deadly eyes that I have ever looked into. They turned my knees to rubber and my heart to stone. In two leaps it could have been upon me but it never moved a muscle, except that its tail was twitching the way a cat's does when it's angry and ready to fight.

"I was afraid to move in case it provoked her to attack. I was still more afraid to stay, but first I must dismount and turn the bicycle and then mount again with all the while the great beast standing there in the road and her cold baleful eyes staring at me.

"I was shaking with fright and the bicycle seemed more awkward and I more clumsy than we had ever been, but finally I was mounted and started for home. I looked back over my shoulder. She wasn't following me. I saw her leap into the bushes south of the road with her kitten and in a moment they had all vanished."

If ever an eastern panther had a child at its mercy it was here, and with the excuse of defending its young for an attack. Yet it stood motionless confronting the young intruder and made no hostile move, even when the terrified girl dismounted from the clumsy bicycle, turned it around, hastily remounted and rode away.

In March of 1947 I started with two companions at daylight to ski the seven miles from our camp to the Bay shore along the Martin Head Road. The road had been closed for the winter and a heavy crust had formed over the three feet of snow on it. A light snow had fallen until about 5:00 a.m., so tracking conditions were ideal.

We had not gone a mile when we came to the fresh track of a large male panther coming out of a heavy black spruce swamp and walking down the road ahead of us. He came to the butt of an overhanging log and paused under it to urinate and scrape. Within a few hundred yards he was joined by a female, accompanied by a one-third-grown cub, and they frisked about on the road together.

We followed the family for about a mile, when they all left the road and entered the very heavy forest in the direction of Point Wolf River. I had by this time exhausted all my film, and had made the most complete set of track photographs of a family group of panthers in existence. We were not equipped to take plaster casts so we had to rely entirely on film.

In July we returned and made plaster casts of the big male's track in soft earth. They were sent to the United States National Museum where they were positively identified as panther tracks by leading authorities. We had proved at long last that the eastern panther was living and breeding in New Brunswick.

At this time one of the men who was with me in March made a trip to the Bay shore and found the tracks of a female and a cub on the sea beach. This cub was smaller in July than the other had been in March, indicating that there were two females with single cubs in the Fundy Hills that year.

In November, calls were heard and two adults and a cub were seen together. Later the two adults were seen together without the cub several times. A man fired four or five shots at one of them at 500 yards with a .30-.30 rifle but observed no hits. A litter from this mating would be born toward the end of April 1948.

In May, a registered guide watched a panther chasing a deer across a road, and on October 25 a panther had a very close call. A deer hunter noticed a panther watching him from a distance of forty yards, and fired at it. The shot raked the belly of the animal and left light-coloured hair over an area of three by five feet. It leaped into the air at least five feet at the shot, and made off. There was no blood to be found, and a bullet mark on a tree showed the shot had gone low. A careful search turned up no trace of the animal. In December another was seen several times about a farm near Cody's, but no damage to livestock occurred.

On November 22, 1951, occurred another of those completely unusual encounters between man and a panther. A panther chased a man out of the woods and he held it off with an axe.

The incident occurred on November 22, 1951, near The Narrows, Queens County, New Brunswick. It is best told by the victim himself. Herman Belyea says: "I was returning home about 6 p.m. I came to a pole fence and before crossing it I hit it with my axe. . . . Within seconds I heard five loud yells off in the woods. . . . I walked about 100 yards further . . . when I heard four or five more yells. I looked back and saw it coming, leaping. I ran a short way when it overtook me, so I had to stop and face it. When I stopped, it stopped and stood up on its rear legs with mouth open and 'sizzling,' and with front paws waving, it charged. I swung the axe at it but it jumped back and I missed, so I ran for it and whooped. It leaped off in the woods and I ran for the house, but didn't run very far before I saw it coming again and had to stop and swing the axe at it. It jumped up to one side so I ran for it and it ran off into the woods again. It repeated the same thing over and over five or six times until I came to a field where I could see the lights of the houses, then it leaped off and never came back.

"The animal was black or dark grey [in the failing light]. Its tail was at least two and a half feet long and it was at least six feet long."

The circumstances of this incident strongly suggest a rabid animal. The loud calls emitted from a distance when the man made a sudden noise show it was not stalking him as prey. It is fortunate the victim was a grown man with an axe. Rabies was unknown in the province at that time, but has since shown itself to be present in wild animals in the region.

In July of 1954 a man with a camera loaded with colour film, and with binoculars around his neck, walked up to within a hundred yards of a panther lying on a down log watching him before he saw it. They stared at each other for about two minutes, the man through his 8x binoculars. Then, while he changed position to get a better angle for a photograph, the panther slid off the log and disappeared. He got no picture, but he had an experience he will long remember.

August brought four more glimpses of panthers along the roads.

They were seen no more that winter, but on October 1, 1955 they made their official debut as members of the fauna of the

74

Fundy National Park. On that day an eighty-pound cat with a two-foot tail showed itself to a Park Warden at Mile 3 on the main highway.

That August (1957) a man got as close as he cared to a full-grown panther. It was on the road to St. Martins and seven to eight miles from the village. Sheldon Snow, his mother, father, wife and two children stopped their car to examine some raspberry bushes on an abandoned farm.

"A large brown animal jumped out of the canes and over a seven foot embankment. . . . I ran to a clearing where the animal had headed and to my amazement a lion went by me about five feet away. I ran after it and it went into the heavy woods and then stopped. I crept along the ground until I was as close as I could get. I studied its body facing away from me, with the head looking back at me, the tail dragging on the ground. I was looking at a full-sized Eastern Panther. I got nervous, but decided to stay and watch. After a few minutes it ran off into the big woods. The body was four feet long—tail, easily three to three and a half feet, dragged on the ground as it stood erect—head small—colour brown—weight 150-200 pounds."

This is the closest observation anybody has yet made of the living animal.

In the summer and fall of 1958 panthers were seen a total of seven times from Grand Lake in the north to the outskirts of Saint John. Two little girls picking berries on an old power line right-of-way flushed a panther that just walked away from them.

"It was big — bigger than a big dog — and it was yellowish in colour and had a long tail. It just walked away from us."

The ex-Chief Forester of New Brunswick, Mr. George Miller, had one cross the road in front of his car, giving him an excellent view of it. It was "a very large brown cat. A splendid-looking animal."

On November 2, 1963, one of the panthers had a very close call. On this date two deer hunters, one a wildlife graduate student at the University of New Brunswick, were hunting south of Grand Lake. They separated, and one was walking across an old field when he heard a growl from a sawdust pile about fifty yards away. A large cat, the colour "of a golden Labrador," was sitting on the edge of the sawdust. He could see only the head and shoulders, and he watched it for about thirty seconds, making up his mind to shoot. He then fired and missed. The panther rose and went down into the bush out of sight. There was an old deer skull where it had been sitting.

"I would never have seen it if it had not growled at me."

That same week, the big male of the Fundy Hills was wounded, how severely we do not know. Two deer hunters were watching a clearing when a panther crossed the opening, climbed onto a woodpile and lay down facing them. They both fired at it and one bullet apparently hit it low in the body.

It fell from the woodpile and lay writhing on the ground. The hunters broke from cover but found there was a deep stream they could not cross between them and the animal. They rushed upstream to the first shallows and crossed, but when they reached the clearing the panther was gone.

Ernest T. Geldart reported: "It was facing us when we fired at it. . . . The animal seemed to be eight or nine feet long and about two feet high and moved very swiftly. It was the colour of a deer, and of massive build. Could see its tail very clearly before it got to the woodpile; also when it was thrashing on the ground. When we fired one bullet could have hit it on the underside of its body as the woodpile was slanted in such a way and one bullet hit directly under it."

A further incident is an unchecked newspaper account of a frightened woman's experience, written some time after the event. I had no opportunity to question the witness. It appeared in the *Times-Globe* of Saint John, New Brunswick, for February 7, 1964. Mrs. D. F. Reid of 253 Prince Edward Street, Saint John, N.B. reported: "I was attracted by the write-up about the lady in East Saint John seeing a black panther in her backyard. I had several experiences two years ago, but rather hesitated writing in about it. I now, even at this late date, feel that I should make it known.

"I moved to the village of Upham in Kings County, where I formerly lived many years ago. I rented a beautiful residence which had been vacated approximately two years before. I paid my rent six months in advance — definitely intending to stay there.

"On the second day I was there, I went to the front door to gaze around and enjoy the lovely trees and fields. That morning I noticed what I thought was a rather tall black stump on the sloping hill right close to the side of the house.

"That afternoon I went out again and to my surprise this stump was gone.

"Next morning I went to the front door again to enjoy the scenery. There was a little pond with a wire fence around it three or four feet high. This was down the slope from the front door, approximately sixty feet — measured.

"I was both surprised and alarmed. Right in view, beside the other side next to the water's edge, was this object similar to what I had tried to convince myself was a black stump.

"I had picked up two or three little white crushed stones in my hand. I tried to convince myself against my better judgment that it was a stump, but just at that time the animal turned its head.

"On the impulse I threw the little stones toward it. I was frightened. The panther turned partly and rose up. To my great horror it sprang right up in mid-air over the fence and glided very rapidly toward me. It touched the ground three times between leaps.

"I staggered back against the double doors, partly falling over the steps. My eyes were on the panther all the time — which only amounted to two or three seconds.

"Strange to say, when it reached where I was, it just gave another spring in the air and bounded under a big tree at the side of the house.

"I feel that the jar of the door made sufficient noise to turn it away.

"It is quite needless to try to express how dreadfully frightened I was. When I recovered a bit, I called some of my neighbours, the forest ranger's family (the ranger was away). Men came. They did not find anything, but measured the distance. Each leap was twenty feet in length.

"I stayed there only three months and although I lost my rent I was too alarmed to stay any longer. I am writing this on purpose to warn the public although a panther may look very shy and docile it is my true opinion it certainly is a very dangerous and treacherous animal; and the public should know that I feel, if it were at all possible, that they should be hunted down so they could not roam around and do harm before it is too late."

Mrs. Reid lost her nerve and her rent. How justified this was cannot be assessed. Certainly a lone woman watching a panther bounding toward her cannot be blamed for her fright. What the panther's intentions were can never be known, but it must be admitted in all fairness that had the panther intended to molest her there was nothing to stop it — but no attack was made. However such an incident does not improve the panther's public image in settled country.

Another observation seems to indicate that a panther was dying of old age and may not have survived the winter of 1965-6. In January of 1966 it was found taking rabbits from snares and it appeared to be partially blind as it crashed into trees and made considerable noise getting through the bush.

At 4:10 p.m. on June 8, 1970, four Park Naturalists of Fundy National Park in Albert County were driving along the main road in the park. A panther crossed the road and jumped the guardrail. They all saw it, and they made plaster casts of its tracks. This spot is about two miles from where I made the original track photographs and casts twenty-three years before in March 1947, but it was the first to be seen in the park since 1959. The vast increase in human use of the area since the establishment of the park drove them out of the immediate area, but they were not far away.

We will close this series of observations by one from a most unimpeachable witness. Minister of Justice and Mrs. J. B. M. Baxter looked out their window in East Riverside, Kings County, at 6:30 p.m. on September 29, 1971. On their lawn, about fifty feet away, stood a long-tailed, tan-coloured cat about the size of a boxer dog, with a dark muzzle. It walked slowly across the lawn and into the bushes. Its limbs were thick. A neighbour said he had seen it also. The same sized animal had been seen in the Fundy National Park on June 13.

This is the end of our tour of the central forests of New Brunswick. It will be seen that panther reports come from all sectors of the circumference. I will leave the reader to judge for himself who was right: Ganong (1903): "not a solitary authentic record, or any other authentic evidence, of either the present or former

occurrence of the panther within the limits of New Brunswick";[1]
or Boardman (1899): "well-authenticated."[2]


Nova Scotia

Let us now consider a very definite recent range extension. Along
the northern fringe of Nova Scotia, from Cape Chignecto in the
west to the Strait of Canso in the east, there lies a belt of rough
hilly country that contains some of the best big game habitat in
the province. It is highest in the central portion where the elevation exceeds 1,000 feet. Beyond the narrow strait the land rises
abruptly again to the highlands of Cape Breton, where the highest point in the province is reached with an elevation of more
than 1,700 feet.

In these rugged regions the highest populations of moose and
deer are to be found, and to the north the western region is divided from the Kent-Westmorland sector of the panther ranges
of New Brunswick by the Isthmus of Chignecto. Deer were not
known in Nova Scotia in historic times prior to 1890, and were
introduced after this date from New Brunswick. These introduc-
tions, aided by natural influx when a northeastward deer invasion
reached the border, built up to one of the highest populations of
white-tails on the continent. With the deer came the panthers.

The first report of what appears to have been a panther in
Nova Scotia was forwarded by the Federal Migratory Bird Officer for the Maritime Provinces, Robie W. Tufts, in 1947. The
events took place twenty-four years earlier in June 1923, but the
witness remembered them clearly. The wife of a farmer in
Pictou County saw the animal five times.

It was seen for a short period and then disappeared, much to
their relief. That summer was a very bad fire year in New Brunswick, and the whole horizon was dull with smoke. Deer were
noted as being exceptionally plentiful in the district. The local
explanation was that there had been an influx of deer from New
Brunswick because of the fires, and "the beast" had come with
them. This is a reasonable hypothesis. Calls suggest a female in
heat, which as we have seen is exceptionally daring. If she found

[1] Ganong, "On reported occurrences by the panther. . . . Bull. Nat. His. Soc.
N.B. 21; 82-6.
[2] Boardman, "St. Croix Mammals," *Calais Times*. 1903. 319-21.

a mate we need look no further for the source of all subsequent reports from this region, even if no more panthers drifted in later from New Brunswick.

Reports then began to come in from widely scattered points in the province. The following are samples selected to show both the spread of the species and the usual ways in which they were seen.

Eighteen years after the Pictou County reports in 1941, and eight miles to the southwest, two men driving near Cards Lake had to stop their car to avoid hitting an animal that stood blocking the road quite fearlessly as they drew up about twenty feet away. It was a cat, much more heavily built than a bobcat (especially in the forequarters), with a long tail that curved down almost touching the road before turning up at the tip.

It looked them over very thoroughly, then leisurely turned its head away and with one twenty- to twenty-five-foot leap it sprang from the centre of the road over a ditch and a four-foot bank and disappeared in the woods.

One of the men was a trapper and hunter with about sixty years experience, and he had never seen a similar animal.

Three years later, and 100 miles farther to the southwest, a most interesting experience took place. In the summer of 1944 four people were driving on the main highway, Route #3, twelve miles west of Shelburne in the southwestern part of Nova Scotia. A small panther crossed the road about 175 yards in front of them, and sat on the side of the road until they came up and stopped, twenty-five feet away. A flock of crows followed it and circled overhead. It showed no fear and sat for several minutes as the observers argued about what it was.

Then one of the men remembered his son's BB-gun, which was in the car. He fired a BB at it and saw the skin of the right foreleg flinch where the pellet hit. It leaped into the air, landed running, and disappeared into the bush.

The animal walked with "a lazy rolling stride similar to an Irish waterspaniel." It was brownish tan all over, and they estimated it was twenty-thirty inches tall. It was one and a half to two times the size of the largest bobcat, a species common in Shelburne County, and its tail was almost as long as its body, sweeping down to the ground and turning up at the tip. They

judged it would weigh at least sixty-five pounds, and they noted the large powerful forelegs. The fact that it seemed quite tame and fearless, together with its size, suggested it was a half-grown cub. Its presence was publicized by the local paper, but it was not seen again. The flock of crows following it may have been the result of a kill nearby, and the placid disposition noted suggests it was well-fed.

This report shows that the species had spread to extreme southwestern Nova Scotia, 200 miles from the region where it was first reported in 1923, in twenty-one years. This is an average of just under ten miles per year. The fact that it was apparently a young animal indicates that there were breeding adults not far away.

A very arrogant individual refused to give way for a man it met walking along the Old Guysborough Railroad in June 1948. It walked steadily toward him and he lost his nerve. When it got too close for comfort he climbed a tree. It kept on walking straight ahead and passed him before turning off into the woods. He had no idea what it was, but said it was what is called "a mountain lion in other places."

The panthers were still in the Pictou County hills. The ex-towerman on the Blue Mountain fire tower saw one in December 1949 in a snowstorm. It had killed a deer nearby and, when he saw it, it was standing looking at him and holding its tail straight up in the air.

In June 1951, a seven-foot panther was seen on a road in the Cobequid Hills, and on September 1, 1952 the first black specimen was recorded from Nova Scotia. It stood for five minutes on the side of the road about ten feet from a man and snarled at him. It had short shiny black hair on its body and tail. Its body was three to four feet long, and it weighed eighty to 100 pounds ("probably nearer 100 pounds"). It had a long tail and a head like that of a wildcat, but much larger. There were young cattle in a pasture nearby, but they were not molested. The man was frightened of it and had no idea what it was. It was reported in the same vicinity in December of 1952, and again in February 1953.

The first account of cubs came in 1951, from the southwestern region of the province. A female and two cubs were reported in the Yarmouth area, and a year later, on August 1, 1952, a fisherman on Lake Annis saw a full-grown adult lying on a rock watching him as he paddled by.

Two other reports that summer indicate there was another family of panthers in the New Brunswick border area. An adult was seen and later a cub was run over but not killed. The driver, a veterinarian, described it as "just like our wild cat with a long tail." It seemed to stand no more than a foot high, but was large enough to make some very noticeable bumps under the car. It was not seriously injured as it bounded off into the woods on the far side. This happened about ten miles from where the adult was seen.

The following year, 1953, a young panther was seen on the road cutting across the base of Cape Chignecto. There was considerable evidence in the form of deer kills that there was a panther in the area, and a calf was killed and consumed, all but the head. The tracks around it were "large and round."

The following year, 1954, a seven-foot panther was reported on the Windsor — Chester road by the Assistant Provincial Forester. A panther had been seen there in 1941, so by 1954 they had been using this district for at least thirteen years.

Two fox hunters saw a panther on the old Chignecto ship railway. They were attracted to loud calls coming from a tree, and found the animal crouched on a branch. They watched it carefully through binoculars and concluded it was "some kind of cat," but unlike any they had ever seen before. It had a long tail and grey and white streaks on its face. It was two feet high and five feet long, and when it called its mouth "looked as big as a soup plate."

Then on March 11, 1954, a resident of Avonport, Kings County, was returning home about midnight when a large animal jumped out in front of his car. He had to stop to avoid hitting it. The next day, L. A. Duncanson, the taxidermist of the Provincial Museum, made plaster casts of the animal's tracks. These were sent to the United States National Museum for identification.

On March 31, 1954 the answer came back from Stanley P. Young, Biologist, Section of Distribution of Birds and Mammals, United States Fish and Wildlife Service.

". . . Regarding the cast from Avonport, there is no doubt in my mind, and this has been confirmed by Dr. H. H. T. Jackson, that these are puma tracks."

Thus was the existence of the panther in Nova Scotia confirmed for the first time.

Across the narrow Strait of Canso from the mainland of Nova Scotia lie the high hills of Cape Breton Island. On the highlands of the northern peninsula are moorlands and subarctic vegetation, existing farther south than anywhere else in Canada. Here the last of the province's caribou lingered, and moose also found a favoured range.

They were gradually restricted to the most inaccessible uplands by the almost unrestricted hunting, and as they disappeared from the lowlands the white-tailed deer took over. Today the caribou are gone, and the moose are mainly to be found in the National Park, where they were reintroduced from Alberta. The white-tailed deer are abundant throughout the rest of the island. On October 14, 1954, a panther was seen crossing a road near Nyanza in Victoria County. The narrow strait had proved an insufficient barrier to bar the great cats from the well-stocked deer ranges beyond.

Five years later, on May 27, 1959, three men were travelling on the Trans-Canada Highway near Kelly's Mountain, again in Victoria County. The highway at this point was under construction. They saw a panther at a quarter of a mile ahead of them and thought it was a deer. They drove up to within forty-fifty feet, and stopped and got out of their truck to look at it. They at once recognized it as a panther. It ran off the road, but then came back across the highway and up a rock cut which was thirty-two feet high. It went up the sheer face of this cut in two bounds and stood at the top looking down at them. They threw stones at it and it growled and hissed.

One man then turned the truck and went two miles back down the road to the nearest camp in search of a gun. The other two stayed and watched it for some time until it entered the woods and was seen no more. It was in sight for about half an hour.

The panther was very unafraid and flicked its paw angrily at the stones they threw at it. The colour was that "of a light deer." The body was four to four and a half feet long, and stood thirty inches at the shoulder. The tail hung to the ground and curled up at the tip. It weighed 135-150 pounds, that is, it was a full-grown adult. The time of the observation was 12:50-1:30 p.m.

In June 1959, a panther was seen between Harrietsfield and Sambro by a man and his two sons. The animal was gaunt-looking, but again showed no fear of the car and allowed an approach to within 200 feet before moving slowly off. It was about a mile from where gaspereau fishermen had left many dead fish on the beach, and it was headed that way. A meal of fish is as attractive to a panther as it is to a domestic cat.

A careful observation of a panther was made by three trout fishermen at Little Loon Lake in Guysborough County on August 14, 1959. At 9:00 a.m. they were crossing the lake to fish on the south shore. The wind was northwest and quite strong. At a distance of about 250 yards they saw a yellowish-brown animal on the southeast shore. They sat very still and watched it through 5x binoculars as they drifted down toward it. It was sitting on a large rock watching them. It saw, heard, and probably smelled them as it was directly downwind, but it showed no fear. Instead it crouched down and drank at the edge of the rock. Then, still crouched, it turned and gave them a long look and entered the woods.

They were able to observe it in three different positions for what seemed to be quite a long time. It was a uniform tawny-yellow, with a black tip to the tail. It finally disappeared when they were 100-150 yards away.

On March 30, 1962, H. A. Macdonald and thirteen other signatories of Sunny Brae, Pictou County, sent the following letter to the Minister of Lands and Forests in Halifax.

Dear Sir,

I am writing to you on behalf of several citizens as well as myself and family appealing to you for direct and immediate attention of a serious situation existing in this village and about this area.

Cougars have been sighted here the past two weeks and as recently as March 25 right in the heart of this village. Cries and calls are being heard at night which may be from the same source. There seems to be no doubt that these wild animals are cougars because they are quite large and have a long tail not associated with any other cat of this size.

... We regard the presence of these animals a distinct hazard to our children and we request that you issue orders to your department employees in Pictou County to take immediate action to try to catch or destroy these animals. We feel there should be no effort spared to get at least one. We have reason to believe there may be several.

... If you fail to heed this request and a child or anyone is attacked in this area as a result, you will bear full responsibility. If you do not see fit to act immediately we will appeal to the Provincial Press by the middle of next week. This is serious and demands urgent measures.

Yours very truly,

H. A. Macdonald
[and thirteen others]

The best bobcat dogs in the province and an experienced cat hunter were dispatched to the area. However their arrival coincided with the spring break-up, and half the country was under water. They gave up after several days of trying, as no fresh sign could be found, and the dogs could not follow a trail if they found it. The panthers apparently moved away. The fearlessness and the calls suggest a mating pair had been in the area.

At this time at least one panther seems to have taken up residence in the Giant's Lake area of Pictou County. On March 19, 1963, the Chairman of the Cougar Committee of the Antigonish Fish and Game Association turned in the following report to the Director of Wildlife Conservation.

"Albert Hattie, August, 1962, Copper Lake.

"Apparently, Mr. Hattie and his dog were in an area of woods in the Giant's Lake Area, when his dog treed a cougar. Mr. Hattie had a very good look at the animal and after realizing what it was, he tied his jacket around the trunk of the tree in hopes the cat would not come down [human scent]. He then left his dog there barking at the cougar and ran home to get his rifle. Upon his return to the tree, he found his jacket and his dog torn to shreds."

The Chairman concluded his report with a request for "at least a dozen special permits for the purpose of hunting these animals down with rifles."

This presents the Department with an almost insoluble problem. If in order to get a permit to carry a rifle in the woods in the closed season all that is needed is a panther report, there would soon be an uncontrollable number of alleged panther hunters roaming the province armed with deer rifles. The report was submitted seven months after the event, so there was no possibility of attempting to follow a fresh trail. Other reports from the area were up to four years old.

It was not until February 27, 1964, that another member of the staff of the Lands and Forests Department saw a panther. The Assistant Provincial Forester had reported a seven-foot specimen on the Windsor-Chester Road in 1941, and in the winter of 1963-64 an aerial moose count was under way in the Antigonish-Guysborough area. A forest ranger was the observer in the aircraft.

They were flying just over the trees along an open hardwood ridge when they came to a large track. They followed it up the ridge and suddenly the ranger saw a large cat sitting in the snow watching them. It had a face "different from a bobcat, a body as long as a deer, and the colour of a boxer dog." As it was on his side of the aircraft and close under them, the pilot could not see it when the ranger tried to point it out. They circled and came over it again, this time on the pilot's side. It ran, and he saw it had a long tail. Thus both pilot and observer combined to give the description of a panther. The forest ranger was familiar with bobcats in the course of his duties, and he had seen the splendid specimens of western cougar in the Provincial Wildlife Park. They were similar to the animal on the ridge.

On March 22, 1964, the snowplough operator from Scotch Village, Hants County, was nine miles from the village on the Watters Road. He observed an animal killing a fawn deer on the road ahead at one-quarter of a mile. It dragged the fawn off the road ahead and began to eat one haunch as the operator watched. Its tracks were three and three-quarter to four inches across, and the animal was heavy enough to sink six to eight inches in heavy snow. The observer called it a cougar.

In June 1964, the Fisheries Warden at North Forchu, Cape Breton Island, heard a commotion in front of his house. He went out to investigate and found that his son and his seventy-five-pound dog had treed a panther about the size of the dog. It hissed at the barking dog. He went for his gun, but the dog was gun-shy and bolted as soon as he appeared with it. Whereupon the panther descended the tree and made off without his getting a shot. It had been seen several times in the area over a period of three months.

During the whole course of this investigation scepticism had been running strong as usual, and nowhere more so than in the senior echelon of the Department of Lands and Forests. Numbers of Nova Scotians had seen the animal and had written to the Department telling of their experiences. A sample of these has been given here. Cubs and mating calls had been seen and heard. Tracks had been seen and photographed, and plaster casts had been made and been positively identified as those of panthers by the world's highest authorities. After that they were returned to the Provincial Museum in Halifax where they are still to be seen. Two members of the Department's own staff, a forest ranger and a senior official, had publicly reported seeing the animal. Yet to the date of writing the official view of the Department is that there is no proof that the panther has ever set foot in Nova Scotia. This extreme scepticism is rather breathtaking. The dead body is all that will be accepted as proof.

Quebec

The great forest of central and northern New Brunswick continues unbroken across the northern border of the province into the wooded hills of the Gaspé Peninsula of Quebec. Until about the 1920's this was moose and caribou country with very few deer. As the caribou moved out of New Brunswick to the south, the survivors withdrew into the uninhabited interior of Gaspé, where the last remnant is to be found today on Mount Albert.

Sir Charles G. D. Roberts was camped with a "new chum" on Upper Squatook Lake to the east of Lake Temiscouata in mid-July, 1885, when they heard an animal calling at night.

In reply to his partner's query about the call "I replied that the voice, in my opinion, came from the dangerous Northern panther, or 'Indian Devil.' These animals, I went on to explain for H's comfort, were growing yearly more numerous in the Squatook regions, owing to the fact that the caribou, their favorite prey, were being driven hither from the south counties and from Nova Scotia."[3]

This statement, published seventy-six years ago by an accomplished bush traveller and naturalist, is revealing. It flatly states what is now thought to have been a recent occurrence — the northward spread of the panther into Gaspé. The statement that the caribou were their favourite prey is also new information which cannot now be substantiated and is doubtful in the light of present knowledge. However, one instance of a caribou kill is recorded in New Brunswick.

The first recent report from this region has not been substantiated, but is unusual enough to warrant mention. Several persons are reported to have seen the bodies of a black bear and a panther that had apparently fought to the death at Lac Côté, Rimouski County, Quebec, in October 1951. In 1958 biologist Claude Minguy tried unsuccessfully to get more details but the trail was then too cold.

In the summer of 1954 the well-known wildlife photographer and outdoor writer Martin Bovey was making a film called "Canada from Sea to Sea." He was driving along the north coast of the Gaspé in August, and was travelling west from the village of Grande Vallée. He was on a gravel road running along a stream where some boys were fishing about a mile from the coast. A full-grown panther stepped out on the road only a few hundred yards beyond the boys. This area is about sixty miles to the northeast of the previous sighting, and shows that panthers had completely crossed the Gaspé Peninsula to the Gulf of St. Lawrence shore by 1954.

[3] Roberts, Sir C. G. D. 1896. *Around the camp-fire.* Thos. W. Crowell and Company. Boston.

89

This record can give heart to those many amateurs who have failed to photograph a panther. Here a professional wildlife photographer, equipped with the best of still and motion picture cameras, was just as unable as any amateur to photograph a large animal he came on unexpectedly when driving on a strange road. It can happen to the best of them.

These records and others (see Appendix I) apparently constitute a recent extension of range. The Squatook report of 1885 is over 100 miles to the west, on about the dividing line between the Gaspé region and the southern Quebec region. They show that today the panther ranges from tide water on the Baie des Chaleurs to tide water on the upper Gulf of St. Lawrence, through the mountainous heart of the great peninsula where it has never before been reported.

The country lying between the St. Lawrence River and the American border is one of the oldest settled in Canada. Panthers had wandered into this area at intervals from the wild hill country to the south with sufficient frequency to have their presence accepted as part of the fauna of the land up until 1863. After this they became more rare and finally disappeared for long periods, as they had in the states to the south.

The skin and skull of a large panther labelled "June 30, 1828, I Loup Cervier or Catamount — from Three Rivers — Donor E. Grième" is now No. 1816 in the National Museum of Canada. Another was chased into a basement in Sherbrooke and shot around 1840. It is No. 1815 in the National Museum.

One was shot by a boy using a nail or spike for a bullet on Croil's Island, on the American side of the St. Lawrence in New York State about 1847. Parts of it are now No. 1814 in the National Museum at Ottawa. Another was shot near Russell-town, Quebec, about thirty miles southwest of Montreal, and presented to the Redpath Museum of McGill University by John Lemming in 1859.

On October 3, 1863 Jacques Gamelin of Baie Lavallières (St. Francis) and two other men were crossing Lake St. Peter in a bateau on their way to Sorel. They were three *arpents* from land (the lake is about nine miles wide) when they met a panther swimming across. It immediately seized hold of their bateau and tried to climb aboard. Being understandably reluctant to allow this, they seized their only weapons, a boat hook and the oars, and proceeded to repel boarders.

C. E. Dionne (1902) tells us that after a lengthy struggle, "during which the animal displayed great obstinacy combined with strength, he was killed, but not before he had succeeded in getting his powerful forepaws on deck. Not being able to make his accustomed spring, in consequence of his hindquarters being under water, he was incapable of injuring either of the men. He fell into the possession of, and was stuffed by, Mr. Craig, the well-known taxidermist."

Coming to this century, a specimen that I have not seen previously recorded in the literature was shot on Mount Royal, November 21, 1909, and mounted by the well-known Montreal firm of taxidermists, The House of Learo. The specimen is still in existence and is vouched for by W. A. Learo. The old excuse that it must have escaped from a circus was used to explain its presence.

The Dominion Bureau of Statistics reports in their "Production of Furs in Canada, Season 1919-1920" that eight panthers were shot or trapped in Quebec that year, and their pelts sold for $5.75 each. This is the last year panthers are mentioned in the fur returns for this province. There is no mention of where they were taken.

Rosarie Morin of St. Zacharie, Quebec, was employed as a guardian of some camps at Little St. John Lake (46° 06′ N, 70° 16′ W) on the Maine-Quebec border in Somerset County, Maine. He had set traps on the Maine side of the lake, and tending them in January 1938 he found a reddish panther caught by the left hind paw. He shot and skinned it, and brought the skin and skull back to his home in St. Zacharie where it was seen by a number of people.

Shortly afterwards Rosarie Morin died and the skin passed into the possession of the village priest. He was naturalist enough to recognize the value of the specimen, and he sent it to Quebec to be mounted. The mounted specimen remained in his possession until his own death, whereupon it became the property of his heir who sold it to the Northeastern Wildlife Station.

The story of how it was discovered may throw some light on other heretofore unknown specimens in this region.

There is some doubt about the exact date. This is the date given by a friend of Morin's who saw the panther. Another friend, who did not see the panther, places it two to three years earlier. I have taken the date the animal was seen.

Wildlife Technician Jacques Normandin of the Quebec Fish and Game Department was investigating a complaint of sheep killing along the border in this area. He was able to show that the sheep-killer was a coyote. One of the local men casually mentioned that that winter he had seen a big cat in the hills, "like the one in the Parish Hall." Very soon Jacques Normandin was looking at the latest specimen of the eastern panther to be mounted in the northeast.

The specimen was crudely mounted, and in an attempt to have it remounted in a different position it was sent to Jonas Bros. of Denver, Colorado, the world-famous taxidermists. They examined it and reported that they would be unable to remount it as it was mounted raw, not tanned, and it would not stand relaxing. This was proof of the local origin of the skin.

As this was the first specimen to reach a tape measure in the long course of this study, its measurements are of interest. It tapes seven feet, one inch in total length, with a three-foot tail. It is mounted in a crouching position and the height at the shoulder is one foot, eight inches. The estimated weight is about 100 pounds. The genitals were removed, but the medium-size, small nose pad, and small head indicate a female. Some hair is missing, and there is some fading, but no sign of the black and white facial markings or the eye-stripes remain. They have apparently faded if they are as distinct in this subspecies as in the western cougar. This is usually a sign of old age, but the state of the teeth and claws indicate an animal in the prime of life.

The specimen is the red colour phase, a uniform red-brown similar to a deer in summer. It is slightly darker on the back, and the tip of the tail is black. The left hind paw, on which the trap closed, has the two central claws missing and there is a trap mark across the toes. The picture shows the specimen as it was originally mounted in Quebec.

The final group of sightings to be considered for this area caused

92

the greatest near-panic this animal has created in history. From about March 7 — April 18, 1959, Canada's largest city, Montreal, was in the grip of a panther scare. Sightings of a group of panthers about the northwest end of Montreal island were covered by the press, radio, television and national magazines. The panthers themselves were never captured, but plaster casts of the foot of one of them was accepted as genuine by two scientists at McGill University's Redpath Museum. Here is what happened.

In the first week of March several people at the west end of Montreal island, where the second of the four mouths of the Ottawa River enter the St. Lawrence, reported seeing a large cat-like animal on the ice of Lake St. Louis. It seemed to be headed for Dowker's Island (or Lynch's Island, depending on which map you use). In the next few days it was seen several times.

At 10:00 o'clock at night a housewife of Baie d'Urfée had gone to the local railway stop to meet her husband coming out from town. She was alone on the platform, but there were several lights. As she stepped onto the platform she saw at the far end a pair of large green eyes reflecting the light. As her eyes got used to the gloom she saw a huge cat crouched on the other end of the sixty-seventy-foot platform. Presently the animal raised its head, then rose to its feet, and stood watching her. She was terrified, but had no place to retreat to, and they stood and eyed each other. The deadlock was broken by the arrival of the train, whereupon the great cat quietly retreated into the bush. Several witnesses reported it as black on other occasions.

On March 14, the first large-scale hunt for the animal (or animals, as for the first time the presence of more than one was suspected) got underway. The area between Ste. Anne de Bellevue and Senneville was covered with no sight of the animals, but tracks were found. Two days later a man who claimed cougar hunting experience in British Columbia appeared and attempted to bait the animals into position to give him a shot, but this too failed. He announced that there were three panthers in the area, one large and two smaller, and that the large one was a male and the two smaller ones females. Based on the known habits of cougars it is much more probable that they were a female with two well-grown cubs, as male cougars do not travel with a harem of females. He discovered the remains of a partridge killed by the two "females."

That day Izaak Hunter opened his column in the Montreal

*Gazette* like this: "No person living has seen the like of what is happening on the island of Montreal this week-end. For, with hounds, rifles, shotguns and bows and arrows several parties will be panther hunting around the west end of the island." The police and first-aid organizations held their breath, but there were no casualties — feline or human.

The hunter who used drawn bait soon gave up and dropped from the hunt when the public arrived en masse to participate. He was probably the only one present who had ever seen a cougar track before.

On several occasions the hounds followed the tracks for some distance, but as they were not allowed to be slipped to run free by police order, to give the still-hunter a chance, they never treed the cats. There were some complaints from the hound men, but most were not too eager to loose their dogs against three panthers. Within the next few days one man lost three out of his four foxhounds he let run outside the prescribed area, which did nothing to raise the enthusiasm of the others, but over 100 hunters took part.

While the still-hunter and others did not succeed in getting a shot at their much harried quarry, they did make plaster casts of their tracks and took track photographs. These were examined by D. J. Cleghorn, Curator of Zoology at the Redpath Museum, and by Dr. Max Dunbar of McGill University. They agreed that the tracks were feline and were too big to be made by anything but a panther.

Ontario offered the use of a helicopter and a crew experienced in running down and shooting wolves with a dart gun for marking, but the hunt lost touch with the panthers. They just disappeared and no more was heard of them, leaving life on the western end of Montreal island to gradually settle back to normal. An event, which was not without parallel in the past, had taken place again. The cats had wandered in early spring across the ice of a great river to the distant shore and found themselves on the most densely populated island in Canada. In the ensuing confusion it took them some time to find their way off again to the safety of the mainland.

They did no damage to man or his animals, beyond frightening the lone woman on the railroad platform, and they left the way they came — unseen, but by no means unsung — and lived up well to the name I coined for them in a previous book, "The Ghost of

North America." Thus ended Montreal's most recent panther hunt.

We now come to the final group of records from Quebec, those north of the St. Lawrence. It is questionable whether these should be called an extension of range, or the reoccupation of a former range. There is only one record prior to this century from this whole vast region, and it is still the farthest north. Seton quotes Thomas Anderson of the Hudson's Bay Company, in saying that an Indian hunter shot a panther on the ice of South Bay of Lac des Quinze in March 1880.[4] He also found where it had killed a caribou. This is about fifteen miles east of the Quebec border opposite the northern end of Lake Timiskaming, and is on the northern fringe of the deer range. If this old record is correct it indicates a panther wandering in the dead of a northern winter, well beyond its normal range, but there is no more reason to disregard it than there is for disregarding the recurring reports from the Yukon border in 60° N. Lac des Quinze lies in 47° 30′ N, and has a climate certainly no more severe than that of the northern Rockies.

Five other reports bring the record up to the late 1960's.

However, before we can accept all records of panthers north of the St. Lawrence as of relatively recent origin, we must not forget the specimen drowned by the crew of the bateau in Lake St. Peter when it tried to climb aboard. This specimen was either heading for, or returning from, the north shore, and the date was October 3, 1863. Also in May 1959, a panther was seen feeding on a deer which had been killed by a car near Temagami, Ontario. It carried the animal off and buried it. This is about forty miles from the South Bay of Lac des Quinze, so panthers may have been in the southern Laurentians for some time.

## Ontario

The last specimen collected in Ontario was sold by Ward's Natural History Establishment to the New York State Museum.

[4] Seton, E. T. 1929. *Lives of Game Animals*. Vol. I. Cats, wolves and foxes. Doubleday, Doran and Co. Garden City. Brantford reprint. Boston. 1953, p. 48.

It was shot "in Ontario, Canada, in 1908," but all further details have been lost. The Ontario reports are given by C. H. D. Clarke in 1970.

The present status of the panther in Ontario is summed up by Dr. C. H. D. Clarke, Chief of the Fish and Wildlife Branch, in a letter dated August 3, 1966.

"There is nothing much to add here, though I am sure that if I had unlimited time, and money for skidoos, aircraft, helicopter charter and the like for a whole winter I could turn one up, and get proof, without killing, for Ontario. Reports worth listening to come from an area from Sault Ste. Marie to the Quebec border. . . . The other area for which I give credence to reports is on the Manitoba boundary. I have always doubted reports east of Port Arthur and around White River simply because there are no deer. If pumas could live without deer, why did they not inhabit the whole north country in the first place? Nevertheless, there is near White River a Mizibishu Lake, with the usual legends. Indians are full of stories about 'Michipeshu' or 'Kechepishu' the great lynx, and the name is given to some of the weird figures on pictographs . . . yet when these Indians moved down to where there were pumas, they applied the name."

Perhaps the 280-mile gap between Sault Ste. Marie and Port Arthur represents the dividing line between the panther of the east and the cougars of the west.

To the west of the New Brunswick panther ranges lies the great roadless forests of northern and eastern *Maine*. My studies have not covered this region and I am indebted to the persons acknowledged in the introduction, and others, for reports from this section. No attempt will be made to present a comprehensive list of Maine records, as they are similar to the Canadian reports we have just seen. They show that the panther is not a newcomer to this area, but has been present but not acknowledged for many years. However, a selection of them is of interest.

In May 1897, Alfred Anderson was a member of a drive crew along Munsungan stream, a tributary of the upper Aroostook River. One night they stopped at a lumber camp where a horse had died the previous winter and had been left where it fell. A panther had been feeding on the carcass and was well-known to the camp crew. Anderson was taken out to see it. He got within forty yards of the panther on the carcass and had all the opportunity he needed to observe it.

Fred J. Farrell, today a retired senior official of the New Brunswick International Paper Company, was a boy of about fifteen years in October 1915. He was living at the village of South La Grange, about ten miles north of Old Town, Maine. Farrell, and several other youngsters of the same age, were in the woods and he had a shotgun. They came across a big cat and Farrell fired at it. It bounded into the woods and disappeared as the youngsters departed in the opposite direction at top speed.

Some days later the body of the cat Farrell had shot was found.

It had spoiled and there was no possibility of saving the skin. By comparing the body with the pictures and descriptions in a natural history book it was identified as a panther. The long tail was unmistakable. This was the same man who sat with me at the fire in Restigouche County, New Brunswick, in 1938.

In late summer of 1948 a lady living on a farm at East Thorndike, Maine, saw what she thought was a man with a white shirt front standing in a patch of raspberries. The "man" disappeared and a panther walked out into the field. She saw it several times, but never again standing on its hind legs.

Early in November of 1949 or 1950, Justice Randolph Weatherbee of the Maine Supreme Court, and Hampden Highlands, Maine, was deer hunting. He and his partner came across tracks in new snow leading to a bushy clearing. The tracks had obviously been made within minutes, and they followed it, "on the chance of seeing the largest bobcat I've ever seen."

When they reached the clearing the animal was on the other side, and interested in something on the road. It was the sound of an approaching truck. As it drew near the animal leaped into a fir thicket and disappeared.

It was as large as Judge Weatherbee's fifty-five-pound Airedale dog but noticeably longer with a long slender tail. It appeared very dark, almost black, but it was wet from falling snow. The distance was paced at 125 feet. The Judge was not convinced at first that he had seen a panther, but after examining various animal plates and texts he decided it could have been nothing else.

At noon on September 10, 1950, Maine State Game Warden Virgil E. Ladd was in Indian Township, Washington County, Maine, about thirty miles west of Calais. He noticed a large buck running toward his car on the Grand Lake Stream Road. About seventy-five yards behind was a panther bounding along in pursuit. When it saw the car it stopped on the road broadside, paused for a few seconds, and then walked off into some thick bushes.

Warden Ladd stopped his car and walked into the bushes after the panther. About fifty yards into the bush he saw a reddish-brown cat about six feet long and twenty-eight inches at the shoulders. It made a whispering noise and waved a long tail at him. He drew his .357 Magnum pistol, aimed at the animal's head, and fired. It leaped thirty feet and disappeared into thick cover as the bullet was deflected by a branch. The track measured four by three and a quarter inches, and a plaster cast was made of it.

Maine State Game Warden Harold W. Green of Vanceboro reported on June 15, 1953, that the day before a panther had come within 100 yards of a woman alone in a field, and screeched. She took off her shoes and ran to a nearby house.

On September 14, 1958, White Nichols of Wiscasset and a friend sketched a five-toed panther track near Spencer Lake in Upper Somerset County. This freak specimen presented the first opportunity to measure the movements of one of these far-ranging cats in the east. A year later the five-toed track was seen and sketched again, this time by a veteran Maine trapper and woodsman, Maurice W. Clark of Milo. The two points where the five-toed animal was found are 100 miles apart, and it is most unlikely there were two freak specimens in the area at the same time.

In concluding the Maine records to the time of writing we can end on a cheerful note. On August 13, 1965, Charles Wilcox of Fredericton was driving from Bangor to Lincoln, Maine. He was between twenty-forty miles south of Lincoln, and it was between

1-2 a.m. He was alone. Suddenly he picked up objects in his headlights ahead, and had to bring his car to a stop. Five panther cubs
were playing in the middle of the highway. They were as large as
"fair-sized pups with the cutest cat faces and golden colour with
long tails."

He sat and watched them for some time, and a jeep came along
with a single occupant from the opposite direction and also
caught them in its headlights. They sat and enjoyed the sight.
Wilcox then remembered me and my study of panthers. The
thought came to him here was a chance to capture a panther cub.
They were of the size that he thought he could hold if he could
throw his coat over it. With this in mind he slowly opened his
door and started to slide out.

A voice from the jeep called out, "Those are panther cubs. The
mother is not far away. Stay in your car!"

And so ended an abortive attempt to capture a cub in Maine
in 1965. Lew Dietz in his book *The Allagash* gives us more Maine
reports up to 1966. A few panthers have been present in this
state for many years, and there is no evidence that they are any
more plentiful than they have ever been. The last observation
tells us they are breeding successfully, so they may be expected to
continue.

The White Mountains of *New Hampshire* are natural panther
country, but they had been thought to be extinct there for about
fifty years. On August 27, 1948, Charles Larned Robinson of
Intervale Farms was driving down the west side of Swift River.
All three persons in the car had a good look at a panther that
crossed the road in front of them. He wrote the North Conway,
New Hampshire, *Reporter*, telling of his experience, and asked if
others had seen the animal.

In the next five days panthers were reported at least three
times.

A party at the Lower Swift River Falls picnic grounds were sitting eating steaks they had just cooked when a very large cat
came out of the woods and stood looking at them. It came up to
within fifteen or twenty feet and they were badly frightened.

On April 29, 1967, New Hampshire became the first northeastern
state or province to protect the species legally and specifically.

On this date a bill originating with Mr. and Mrs. Horace Hudgman of Concord, and sponsored by Republican Representative George Kopperel of Loudon and Canterbury, was signed into law.

Moving westward from New Hampshire into the State of *Vermont*, two of the best panther records come from the fire tower lookout on Gore Mountain in the northeast corner.

Gore Mountain Fire Tower,
Essex County, Vermont,
Late August, 1948.

To:   Mr. Bruce S. Wright
From:  Walter Harlow
Subject:  Panther seen in daylight

"Time: 1700 hrs. E.D.S.T. Place: From about fifty feet above ground. Distance to specimen, about 100 feet. Portion seen: From left ear to the rear.

"The animal was motionless for upwards of three minutes. Colored like deer at that season. Powerful shoulders est. eleven to twelve inches across. Long cylindrical tail, extending perhaps eight inches parallel to ground behind heels. Observer felt he was being conservative in estimating weight at 125 pounds. Well-nourished, healthy-looking specimen, well-groomed in appearance.

"Interested itself in deer trails (proximity to junction of four).

"Observer had visual aid of binoculars (Bausch and Lomb, 7 x 35)."

Also from Walter Harlow came the following report.

"Subject:  Panther seen in sunlight.
Time 0800-0900 hrs. Place: from ground level. Distance to specimen: about sixty-five feet. Position of specimen: Head-on. (The animal was watching the observer's cabin. The long axis of the animal's body nearly coincided with the observer's line of vision.) Motion: that of long tail swishing laterally behind the heels. Duration of observation: A little over two minutes. Termination: The animal swung to its left and leapt a twenty-eight-inch

101

stump and disappeared. Color: Tawny. Darker above to lighter underneath. Adult. Body length estimated above four feet. Height at shoulders about twenty-five inches. Came to point of visibility on a deer trail."

Claxton Brown of New Britain, Connecticut, watched a panther lying under some trees behind a cemetery at Randolph, Vermont, for about forty-five minutes on April 2, 1963. He got up to within sixty feet of it and threw snowballs to make it move. It seemed very tired and wanted to lie up for the day and was reluctant to leave.

He went for help in the form of men with dogs and guns. When they arrived some hours later the panther had gone. The dogs became interested several times but were unable to unravel its trail over the hard crust that supported the men and the panther.

Spargo (1950) points out that the panther was never numerous in Vermont. The number of panthers shot in the state in the more than 200 years since the first white men entered the region does not number a score. Authentic killings since the last third of the eighteenth century are less than half that many, and even vague and uncertain reports would add less than as many more. He points out that for every panther killed, there were 500-1,000 reports of panthers seen. Notwithstanding this fact, some of these reports were true and proof was furnished by the bodies of the dead animals. He concludes that there is nothing inherently impossible in the claim that a panther has been seen in the Vermont woods today, and there are a number of people who would agree with him, although the last specimen killed was taken near Barnard on November 24, 1881.

The Adirondack Mountains of *New York* State were prime panther country in the early days of settlement, and the species occurred in other parts of the state also. As elsewhere, it was quickly exterminated in the settled areas, and any survivors were driven into the mountains. The depletion of deer following settlement probably contributed more to the panther decline than did direct hunting.

Deer management has reached a high level in the state today,

103

and the present herd is probably as large as the pristine population, if not larger. The stage is therefore set for the return of the panther, and reports of them being seen again are reaching the Conservation Department. So far no recent specimen has been taken.

To the east of southern New York lies the State of *Massachusetts*, abutting on the north on Vermont and New Hampshire. This is heavily settled country and would appear most unsuitable for panthers. Nevertheless they have been reliably reported there recently. In 1953 two were seen in South Royalston on the New Boston road. They were hunted with untrained dogs who either lost them or gave up after one of their number was mauled. This was directly south of Little Monadnock Mountain, a short distance over the border in New Hampshire.

There were occasional reports over the next few years, and on February 13, 1960, Conservation Officer Roland D. Gaudette of Mountain Lakes followed the tracks of two panthers for one and a half miles in the towns of Groton and Dunstable, Massachusetts. The tracks in snow measured six inches across, and he was photographed holding one upon his return.[1] The tracks were a day and a half old, and the animals were apparently hunting, as they investigated brush piles and went around and under open camps.

Conservation Officer Gaudette estimated there were twenty reliable reports of the animals that had apparently been in the district at intervals for at least two years. One report told of seeing a panther kill a raccoon. Another was from a farmer who had left a still-born calf at the back of his field intending to bury it the following morning. During the night he heard "an awful noise" and his dog "was going crazy." He took a light and went out and saw the form of a large animal with very big eyes. The next morning the calf was gone.

The panthers stayed in one general area for a time and then disappeared for two or three months. They were heard calling at night on a number of occasions. When this happened all the dogs within earshot began to bark.

On November 15, 1960, an incident occurred on the Massachusetts Turnpike, about seventy miles to the southwest, that may

[1] *Outdoor Maine*, June 1960, page 17.

shed some light on the wanderings of one of these panthers. Four people were driving from Albany, New York, to Westfield, Massachusetts on the turnpike at 7:45 p.m.

When they were twenty minutes west of #3 Exit an animal came down the embankment between the eastbound and west-bound lanes and stepped out onto the road in front of them.

Harry N. Donaldson wrote to say: ". . . An animal which I feel I must call a mountain lion, came down the embankment . . . and out onto the pavement. . . . Rather than hit it with only one wheel, avoiding it was impossible, I hit it dead center. The impact was noticeable, in fact it fractured the license plate frame, and the car passed over it. It is my opinion that no animal struck in this manner could possibly have survived. This occurred at 7:45 p.m. and was reported to the attendant on duty at the toll booth at exit #3 at 8:05 p.m.

". . . I say I must call it a mountain lion, for the following reasons. I spent two years in Arizona and saw three mountain lions there. Two alive, and one that I shot. . . ."

The maintenance crew could not find the body, so it must have crawled off the turnpike. Mr. Donaldson told his story to a member of the New York State Conservation Department, who ridiculed him, and on December 9, 1960, sixteen days later, he wrote to me. I passed his letter to the Massachusetts Co-operative Wildlife Research Unit at the University of Massachusetts, as worthy of immediate investigation, but by this time two feet of snow had fallen and the quest was abandoned. Thus probably died a panther a short distance from the Massachusetts Turnpike in 1960.

It appears likely that there have been two panthers in the Quabbin Reservation of Massachussetts in 1968-9. If they are a mated pair they may settle down and stay for some time, if not molested.

While on the subject of turnpikes, and to include another state in this survey, I will give here a panther record which was made thirty-two and a half miles from New York City, in the State of *New Jersey*. Dr. William V. Garner reports: "Last Sunday night [late May, 1958] at 10:30 p.m., my wife, two children and I were returning to Long Branch from Philadelphia. As it was raining, shortly after passing the toll gate (on the Garden State Parkway) we entered a slight curve in the road. The headlights of the car picked up a large tan-coloured animal standing about forty feet east of the highway. My immediate reaction was that it was a deer. . . . As we went past, however, the 'deer' turned out to be a puma! I was so completely stunned that I kept going (about 35 m.p.h. as it was raining). Another car, however, about fifty yards behind us, had entered the curve, and the puma was picked up in its headlights. Before I could inform my wife what it really was, she exclaimed, 'That was no deer. That was a lion!' We both had an excellent view of the animal, despite the rain. It was between five and six feet long, tan-colored, with a long, uniform black-tipped tail. I have seen the puma in the San Jacinto Mountains of southern California and feel, since I have four earned degrees in Biology (Ph.D.—University of California, Berkeley) that I am qualified to distinguish a puma from a deer, large boxer, zebra, etc."

On reaching home Dr. Garner attempted to find out if any zoo or circus had lost a puma, and called the local paper. No animals were missing, and his report was treated with ridicule. Not even "four earned degrees in biology" saved him that, and he quickly dropped the subject.

In the fall of 1967 the State of *Connecticut* recorded two panther sightings. A bus driver in West Rock reported one walking down a quiet street, and the police turned out and searched the area without trace. Soon after, near Branford, State Senator Lucy T. Hammer and her husband were having breakfast when a panther walked quietly past their house. It walked down their path and into the woods. A search turned up only a dead squirrel which had been sliced in half.

*Maryland* recorded a sighting on August 26, 1971.

To the west lies the type locality of the eastern panther, the State of *Pennsylvania*. For long years the late Colonel Henry W. Shoemaker of Harrisburg was the panther authority of this state, and in this section I will draw upon his records.

The numbers of panthers present in Pennsylvania in the early days of settlement seem almost beyond belief today. In 1760 almost 200 hunters set out to form a circle about thirty miles in diameter, covering most of Snyder County. They converged to the centre, killing the game as they went.

The bag for the drive showed "41 Panthers, 109 Wolves, 112

106

Foxes, 114 Mountain Cats, 17 Black Bears, 1 White Bear, 2 Elk, 98 Deer, 111 Buffaloes, 3 Fishers, 1 Otter, 12 Gluttons, 3 Beavers, and upwards of 500 smaller animals."[2] Probably twice as many panthers escaped as were killed.

The last panther on which a bounty was paid in Pennsylvania was shot in the Moshannon region of Center County in 1886, but Shoemaker gives a list of annual sightings up until 1942. He points out that this list is selected as most interesting from a large number of reports available, and concludes, "... the weight of evidence weighs heavily that *Felis concolor*, the king of Pennsylvania beasts, has been here, and probably still passes through, on his old migration paths, in Governor James' fair Commonwealth, 1942."[3]

Several interesting points come out of these records. The first is that a number of observers describe the animal as shiny black. In two cases the animal was seen in water. A man was fishing a small creek at night. He heard something wading down the stream, but he paid no attention as he thought it was his companion who was fishing above him. The sound stopped just short of him, and he turned to speak to his friend. He found himself looking into the eyes of "a huge black panther." He ran up the bank yelling for his friend, and the panther crossed the creek and headed for the mountain. Within two hours, armed men with fox and coon hounds were on the scene and the trail was found, but once again the dogs refused to give chase.

In the second instance the panther swam across a large pond after being fired at.

On two occasions an odd feeding habit has been observed, indicating that natural food is scarce in the area. Panthers were twice seen to feed on bread, still in the wrappers, left at picnic sites in state forests.

As no one believed there could be such a thing as a black panther, a reporter referred to it as "the critter," and the name stuck. At first it was believed to be an escapee from an animal show, but later sightings indicated there was more than one animal in the

[2] Seton. 1929. Quoting Shoemaker.
[3] Shoemaker, Col. H. W. 1943. "The panther in Pennsylvania," Penn. Game Comm. Harrisburg. 13(11). Feb.

107

area. About 1953 the Lycoming County Consolidated Sportsmen's Association organized a large "Critter Hunt," which became an annual event. But as Mr. Watts, a Justice of the Peace, points out, "As luck would have it, it has either rained or snowed on every 'Critter' day. Even so, hundreds of men have taken part, but to date not one 'Critter' have they killed."

In closing the Pennsylvania reports I will give two undated news items that were sent to me at this time.

"AFTER THE LAST PANTHER IN PENNSYLVANIA, 1954. *700 Hunters Set To Track Critter of Cogan's House.* Williamsport—An estimated 700 hunters are expected to join Saturday in the hunt for a black panther believed to be roaming Bobst Mountain twenty miles northwest of here. Plans for the hunt were made when reports reached here that tracks of a large cat had been found in Cogan House Township. President Judge Charles Scott Williams, of the Lycoming County courts, is chairman of the hunt for the 'critter of Cogan House Township.' Dozens of other country officials and prominent sportsmen of the state are behind the hunt. Many sportsmen of the region believe some sort of 'critter' is at large, attacking livestock and killing small game. A cash prize of $300 will be paid to the killer of the animal, and other prizes are being offered for those bagging foxes and wildcats."

*The Mount Carmel Item*
"Critter is seen near here

"The 'critter' that has been terrorizing Cogan House Township in Lycoming County for the past several weeks, has been reported seen on the Aristes road, between Centralia and Aristes, according to information prevalent over the week-end. Joe 'Duke' Smith, resident of Centralia, said in town today he had seen a 'critter' he described as a black panther two feet high crossing the Aristes road on Friday night. Hundreds of hunters, trappers and woodsmen have been haunting the forests on Bobst Mountain, twenty miles northwest of Williamsport, in an effort to track down the animal, believed either to be a black panther, a mountain lion or a large bobcat. Volunteer patrol planes, mobile Red Cross units and various other agencies have been enlisted in the hunt for the 'critter' which has frightened game away from the popular hunting grounds of the Lycoming area."

With all this disturbance the panthers left the area. The massive hunt got nothing despite the large reward placed on the head of the rarest animal in the state.

Then on October 28, 1967, occurred an event that was unique in the region for many years. A panther, or a mountain lion, was killed near the town of Edinboro in northwestern Pennsylvania. John Gallant was hunting squirrels when he saw a large cat. He departed for reinforcements and returned with men and dogs. They treed and shot the cat. It was an immature female, too young for the subspecies to be identified, even by the Curator of Mammals of the Carnegie Museum who examined it.

Beyond establishing that there were no cage marks or collar marks on the dead cub, and no other evidence that it had ever been in captivity, nothing more could be learned.

If this specimen had been sufficiently mature to have had its subspecies identified it would have answered the question: Is the eastern panther extinct in the United States? Unfortunately we must wait until a mature specimen is presented to a trained biologist to get the answer.

In closing out the evidence from Pennsylvania it is worth quoting the last two paragraphs from the short paper on this specimen delivered to the American Society of Mammalogists in an annual meeting at Fort Collins, Colorado, on June 18, 1968, by J. Kenneth Doutt, Curator of Mammals, Carnegie Museum.

"Two sections in western Pennsylvania have produced so many reports over the past fifteen years or so that I am convinced there must be some mountain lions living there. Could it be a small breeding population?

"Where there is so much smoke there must be some fire, and I think it is time we took a careful look at the evidence."

In the 650 miles from Pennsylvania to Florida there lies the empire of the southern mountains, the pine forests, and the moss-draped cypress jungles of the coastal lowlands. Such names as the Great Dismal Swamp and Okefenokee bring to mind great areas of water-soaked land, winding between the knobby cypress trees, as tiny pirogues are poled along canals, and clouds of water birds circle overhead. Inland the pine forests of the Piedmont merge into the mountain forests of the Blue Ridge, and all of this is panther country.

No attempt will be made here to enlarge on the work of the

late Herbert Ravenel Sass of Charleston, South Carolina, who was the chronicler of the panther in the *southeast*. He amassed a great amount of data which was passed to me at his death by his widow. The best of it appeared in his "The Panther Prowls the East Again!" in the *Saturday Evening Post*. It will suffice here to select points of major interest in the behaviour of the animal and its relations with man that have appeared in this region.

Sass began his search for the panther in the southeast amid the peaks of the southern Appalachians, which rise to over 6,000 feet. He reasoned that it would be here that a fugitive from civilization would be most likely to be found. He talked with the oldest inhabitants, both Indian and white, and he heard many tales of Klandaghi, Lord of the Forest. Everywhere he went he was told that the splendid beast had passed from their world long ago. At last, discouraged by the sparse mountain wildlife he found, he returned to his native low country where by comparison wildlife teemed. Here he was not long in striking the trail he sought.

One night in the fall of 1948 the manager of the Rice Hope Plantation on the Santee River was making a routine anti-jack-lighting patrol with a helper. They drove a truck to the suspected area and then proceeded on foot. The manager carried a .22 rifle, but the other man was unarmed. They had not gone far when they heard "a queer sound" ahead, and the manager switched on a flashlight.

In the beam he saw a huge cat, "like a maneless lion," rear slowly up on its hind feet and stand erect like a bear. (Remember the lady at East Thorndike, Maine.) Its long tail removed all possibility that it was a bobcat distorted by the light. Its eyes were on a level with his own, and it weighed at least 160 pounds.

Speaking over his shoulder, and not taking his eyes off the cat, he asked his companion whether he should try to shoot it with the .22 rifle. He got no reply. A few minutes later he heard the truck door slam. He lost no time in reaching it himself with his rifle still unfired.

Just before Christmas, 1951, a panther leaped from a tree onto the roof of the large rambling Lucas house on the Kinloch Plantation, again in the Santee River area. It was at night and the sound was "as if a horse had been dropped from 100 feet onto the tin roof." It walked about the roof with the moon behind it, giving the observer a good opportunity to see its long tail. After

110

exploring the roof it took a flying leap into a nearby oak tree, and disappeared into the shadows of hanging moss.

Turning now to the last region that will be considered where the panther has survived east of the Mississippi and north of Florida, we come to the State of *Alabama*.

In this state the panther is definitely established as part of the local wildlife, and here, at long last, we find a hound that knew her job. On March 16, 1948, farmer A. D. Hare was taking down a pasture fence a mile west of Ashville in St. Clair County. With him was his hound Queen. She started baying at something concealed in the grass and he went to investigate. As he approached, a panther sprang from the grass and fled to the nearby woods with Queen in hot pursuit. Hare ran for his house and a 12-ga. shotgun.

Queen had the panther treed when he returned, but it jumped from the tree and ran when it saw him. He fired at it twice, but as he only had bird shot in the gun, it kept on going. However, it was hit and Queen brought it to bay against a bank and held it until he arrived. After some manoeuvring he shot it in the back of the head and killed it. It was mounted and is on display in Birmingham today.

Two or three sightings a year reach the Game and Fish Division of the Department of Conservation, which makes no special effort to collect them. The panther is accepted as a resident of the State of Alabama and may be expected to continue in low numbers for a long time to come.

The panther is estimated to number 50-100 left alive in Florida, and is regularly recorded in Louisiana and Arkansas. Arkansas is, of course, west of the Mississippi River, but the panther population there is more closely affiliated to the east than to the west.

The animal is making a slow comeback in the southeast as well as in the north.

The evidence here presented suggests that panthers exist today from the Laurentians to the Everglades of Florida, and from Nova Scotia to Louisiana. Over all of this great range their population level must be the merest fraction above total extinction.

111

Yet only in two states, New Hampshire and Florida, of this vast region does man offer a helping hand. They are unprotected "varmints" everywhere else, and any individual or organization is at liberty to put a price on their heads at any time. As we have seen, this has actually been done. This is the state of affairs governing the survival of one of the best examples of evolutionary perfection in the conservation-minded North America of the 1970's.

# Chapter 4
## The animal

The first question usually asked when panthers are under discussion is, "How big are they?" Emmons reports a large individual, presumably a male, from New York as having a total length of nine feet.[1] This is as large as any of the western subspecies, although larger specimens have been reported from South America. The maximum published weight for a puma in North America is 276 pounds, "after the intestines had been removed."[2] This was an eight foot, seven and three-quarter inch specimen from Arizona, killed in March 1917. The females are considerably smaller in both length and weight.

It appears therefore that the eastern panther may be anything up to nine feet long and 280 pounds in weight. Tracks I have photographed and made plaster casts of in New Brunswick suggest that there are individuals alive today as large as any in the west. These sizes and weights seem to be the extremes, as Hornocker in Idaho found that mature females averaged about 100 pounds and mature males about 150 pounds in weight. How large will *Felis concolor* grow in an abundant food supply where it is not hunted? With deer in North America, the largest specimens are found in the northern regions and the smallest in the Florida Keys. The big grey Alberta lions appear longer than the Florida panther. Yet in North America, a nine-foot specimen is quite unusual.

When we look at South America, the distribution of size in the

[1] Emmons, E. 1840. *Report on the quadrupeds of Massachusetts.* Cambridge, Mass. 86 pp.
[2] Roosevelt, Theodore. 1901. "With the cougar hounds." Scribner's Mag. 30(4). Part 1: 417-435, 434; Oct; Part 2: 545-564, 556. November.

puma seems to be the same. The largest specimens are reported from the far south, and they appear to considerably exceed the largest from North America. A letter from J. W. Edmond, who spent most of his long life as a sheep rancher in Patagonia, remarked that he has shot "many" over ten feet in length. He submitted a picture of his largest, which he says measured eleven feet, two inches from tip to tip. It was shot in the Valley of the Cows, Patagonia, on January 17, 1907. In North America this species is not measured by total length for record purposes, but by skull measurements, so no direct comparisons are available, but this specimen appears to greatly exceed the known world's record. It appears to be only exceeded in length by the Siberian tiger, which is also a pereferal subspecies. It should be noted, however, that in 1872 when Florida was very wild Charles J. Maynard said of the local panther: "It is quite a formidable animal, growing sometimes to eleven feet in length."[3]

If these measurements are correct, the Patagonian pereferal population appears to have run to gigantism over the norm of the species. Before the coming of the sheep and rifle-bearing sheepherders to this region, the cats' only predator was the native Indian who was inadequately armed to successfully hunt this formidable animal. The Indians were probably only an incidental cause of mortality, and were by no means a population control. Therefore the pumas of Patagonia in those days probably lived out their life span amid an abundant food supply, and attained their full-growth potential.

With the coming of the rifle-bearing sheepman, the native animals were soon eliminated and the sheep replaced them as the pumas' main food. This sealed their doom, and it is improbable that any of these giants are alive today. They are hunted down before they reach full size. This seems to be born out by the largest specimen listed by the most recent work.[4] The animal had a total length of eight feet, two and a half inches, and was an adult male. That is why Mr. Edmond's account and his pictures are unique.

Thus we see that the tigers of the world reach their maximum size on the northern edge of their range in the northern hem-

[3] Maynard, C. J. 1872. "Catalogue of the mammals of Florida, with notes on their habits, distribution, etc." Bull. Essex Inst. 4(9-10): 2-3.
[4] Cabrera, Angel. 1961. *Los felidos vivientes de la Repúblic Argentina.* Mus. Arg. Cience. Nat. Ciencias Zool. TVI. No. 5. Buenos Aires. 247 pp.

isphere, but do not extend beyond the tropics in the southern hemisphere. The pumas, on the other hand, range to the extreme edge of the temperate zone in both the northern and southern hemispheres, and here they reach their maximum size in both places.

We know so little of the life history of the species in the east that we must rely on information collected from other subspecies in different parts of the continent. By amending this information as indicated by the climate of the northeast we arrive at our best guess as to how our panthers live. In the west the animal is polygamous, but this is much less likely to be so in the extremely sparse and scattered population in the east. Monogamy would appear to be much more likely here.

The females mate for the first time between two and three years in the west, and there is no evidence of anything different here. The males do not reach sexual maturity until they are somewhat older. The female tends the young alone until they are at least old enough to accompany her. If the male finds young cubs alone in the den he may eat them, so the female's concern is well-justified at this age. Later the male is allowed to join the family and perhaps help her provide food.

From one to five young are born after a gestation period of about ninety days. Larger litters are known, but five is the largest number usually raised. One such litter was seen in Maine in 1965.

An expanding population of cougars has an average of three or four cubs per litter. They may be born at any time of the year, but in the north those born in spring and summer have the best chance of surviving the winter weather conditions and food scarcity. The cubs stay with the mother for up to two years in the wild, but I once saw a young male in a zoo nursing when he was larger than his mother. I have in my office the skin of a young male from Vancouver Island which was shot in company with an adult female, presumably his mother. His skin is seven feet long.

How much country is required to support a fully-grown panther? Adult males have a regular territory, or home range, which usually contains more than one female.

The latest study,[5] and the only one to use marked individuals,

[5] Hornocker, M. G. 1969. "Winter territoriality in mountain lions." *J. Wild. Mgmt.* (33)3: 457-464.

was done in Idaho by Hornocker. He found that the smallest winter range of a female during one season was approximately twenty-five square miles. The males generally occupied larger territories of fifteen to thirty square miles. Their territories did not overlap, as did those of the females, but they did overlap those of the females. No evidence of territorial defence could be found, and fighting between individuals seemed to be almost nonexistent.

Hornocker found that they actively avoided each other, and mutual avoidance behaviour operated to keep them apart both in space and time. Markers (scrapes) that could be detected both by sight and scent were used to avoid encounters, but transients of both sexes moved freely through the occupied territories. At the end of five years of study, Hornocker estimated that there were not more than ten full-time adult residents of his 200-square-mile study area in winter.

It is fascinating to note that the Bengal tiger, an animal that grows to twice the weight of the puma, also requires only twenty-five to thirty square miles of hunting range. The giant Manchurian tiger, the world's largest cat, measuring over ten feet and weighing up to 700 pounds, is the only one that requires more space.

How do panthers kill their prey? Adult cougars rarely hunt by lying in wait. This is usually done by young animals just learning to kill their own food. The adults hunt by stalking their prey to within a distance they can cover in two or three leaps and then springing on it. They hunt as much by day as at night, in the western ranges. If the prey is a deer it is hit high on the shoulder and neck, and the canine teeth are set into the back of the neck or the base of the skull. The muzzle may be seized by one paw and bent back, as the shock of the charge bowls the deer over. This combination of impact, bite and twisted head usually results in a clean kill with a broken neck. This however is by no means always the case, and it takes considerable practice before the panther becomes proficient at it. Younger, less skilled animals may kill by strangulation.

One method of killing a deer was seen and photographed in the Florida Everglades. The observer was watching for one of the small, south Florida white-tailed bucks to come into a clearing. He was sitting on a big leaning cypress log with a large slab

116

of bark at his back. Instead of his buck, a small doe stepped into the clearing and began feeding on mushrooms and fern buds.

He took out his camera and was photographing the doe when he noticed a panther emerge from the forest beyond and crouch down watching her. Within seconds the panther charged, and the doe saw it and ran just before it reached her.

The panther made a "gigantic running lunge" and buried the claws of one paw in the doe's withers. It seized the face with the other paw, and at the same time bit into the back of the neck. They both went down, and on the ground the panther changed the position of its paws. It wrapped both forearms around the doe, and held her to its chest as it delivered several severe downward-raking double kicks of the hindpaws to the doe's spine. This, combined with the teeth in the back of the neck, killed her as the bleating stopped, and the panther released its hold and stood up.

Then, apparently having no wish to eat at the moment, the panther scraped leaves and litter over the kill with one foreleg, and disappeared into the forest. The observer was apparently never seen by the panther, and he went home with the finest set of photographs of a panther kill ever made.

An unusual kill was made in New Brunswick in 1969. A forty-pound pig was killed within twenty yards of a house on the Oromocto Indian reservation. It was a noted squealer and was kept in a pen alone. There were several loose dogs about. One night the dogs all barked frantically and chased something away from the pigpen. The pig was found dead.

It had been killed instantly, and before it could squeal, by a bite across the back of the neck just behind the ears. The holes made by the canine teeth of the killer were two inches apart. The only other marks on the pig appeared on its back and side, and were faint claw marks. The unusual thing about them was that only one claw penetrated the hide. It went in deep and entered the body cavity. From the position of the teeth marks on the neck this was apparently the left forepaw, which had only one functional claw.

I made plaster casts of cat tracks three and a half by three and a half inches, in the pigpen.

The dogs had jumped the cat from its kill before it had had a chance to begin eating and before it could carry it off. I warned the owners that the killer would probably return for the pig that night as it was still hungry, and for them to tie up the dogs and let it carry off the pig. We would then follow it up and shoot it as it had shown itself to be a stock killer. However this advice was not followed and the dogs were again left loose.

The cat returned as predicted and was promptly chased off for the second time by the dogs, before it could reach the pig. It did not return. Over an inch of rain fell that day and attempts to follow it up were unsuccessful.

It is probable that we have a panther with a maimed forepaw which has only one claw left in this area. The injury may have been the result of an escape from a trap, and is probably why it killed a pig so close to civilization. It may no longer have been able to kill deer. Fortunately there was a hare population high in the area at that time, and the panther did not molest domestic stock again.

After a deer is dead the hair may be clipped and licked off an area of the rib cage, and a hole opened through which the liver and heart are eaten. The kill is then disembowelled, and the meal proceeds. If the cougar intends to return for another meal, the kill may be covered by scraping snow, leaves or ground litter over it. I have observed all these operations in New Brunswick, so presumably the eastern panther follows a similar course. This may be called the typical procedure, but there seems to be considerable variation.

The main food of the animal anywhere is apparently deer, but almost any other animal, bird, fish or amphibian that they can catch will be taken. In the east this includes woodland caribou (but not moose), beaver, raccoons, snowshoe hares, porcupines, ruffed and spruce grouse, trout and frogs. Mice have been recorded in the west, and as a panther has been seen digging in a field in the east they should apparently also be included here.

Farther south, feral hogs are an important addition to their food and the grouse are replaced by wild turkeys, which are vulnerable because of their roosting habits at night. Opossums replace porcupines, and the swamp rabbit replaces the varying hare. In the mangrove swamps of south Florida the panther preys on raccoons, foraging on the beach at low tide.

Stoner gives an interesting old account of the lengths a panther will go to get fish.[6] A trapper in the Adirondacks and his partner were preparing their camps for winter. One of them went fishing, and secured a string of trout which he tied out in the stream. He started up-stream to the next pool, leaving his rifle below the string. He took a large trout and then, remembering his rifle, he turned back to get it.

He was in time to see a panther spring from the opposite bank of the first pool into the water, grab the string of trout and emerge on his side. The panther was now between him and his rifle. He threw the large trout he had just caught into the water above the panther, and it leaped after it. This gave him the chance to reach his rifle and shoot the panther. This took place before 1837.

Panthers have been recorded stealing hams and sides of beef from lumber camps. They have also been seen eating the offal of a dead horse, a butchered cow, and chickens killed for market. They have been known to have carried off a still-born calf. The most unusual instance is the report of panthers eating bread in the wrappers left by picnickers.

Like all predators, panthers will eat what is available, and there is no question of going hungry until a preferred species comes along. A hungry panther searching for fresh meat and blood will take what first comes its way. It is not hunting "for deer" or "for grouse"; it is hunting for food of any description.

The female panther has but one main requirement—food— and if she can find it all year round in one area she will stay there. Once she is mature, sex only enters her life at two- or three-year intervals. On the other hand, the male has two main requirements—food and sex—at all times. He may be able to find enough food in one area to support him all year round, but as any one female will only accept him every two to three years, he is constantly on the move, searching for other females coming into heat and eager to accept him. Thus the home range of the male may be considerably larger than that of the female.

The minimum-sized home range necessary to support west-coast cougars can be deduced from the fact that they sometimes swim out to the offshore islands. They have been known to stay on these islands, which are three to seventy-five square miles in

[6] Stoner, D. 1950. *Extant New York specimens of the Adirondack cougar.* Circ. 25. N.Y. State Mus. Albany. May.

120

area, for as long as a year, but they eventually leave. Apparently such an area is not sufficient to support them in these islands.

The panther in the east does most of its hunting at night, or in the late evening and early morning. The large eyes are admirably adapted for seeing in dim light. The sense of smell is used in addition to sight, and panthers have been seen following the trails of deer and rabbits. A panther will kill rabbits, grouse and other small prey by blows of its paw, but when it attacks a deer this is the supreme test of its skill as a predator.

The rate of killing by pumas has been the subject of much discussion. Estimates have ranged from a deer a week to a deer every two or three months. There seems to be no satisfactory answer, as it depends entirely upon the quantity of other food available.

Deep snow may actually be an asset to a panther living on deer. The panther, with its large-padded paws, is at less of a disadvantage than the deer.

The willingness to return to an old kill in a cold climate with only a fair food supply is shown by an observation made in New Brunswick. In January 1952, a buck deer had been killed, partly eaten, and buried in the Juniper area. On April 11th the tracks of two panthers, a mother and her last year's cub, were found in the area. The tracks led straight to the deer kill, which was dug up and cleaned out. Even the leg bones were licked clean. The location of the kill was apparently well-known to the female, suggesting it was her own.

Damage to domestic stock is so slight in the east as not to be worth mentioning when discussing food habits of the panther. Even in British Columbia, where cougars are most numerous, these losses are very low.

It is not yet clearly understood whether the cougar or the panther are selective in their hunting. Certainly they do not appear to make any special effort to seek out the sickly. They kill the deer that gives them the best opportunity, which may well turn out to be the young and the old. Hornocker found[7] that in Idaho the mountain lions killed a greater portion of young and

[7] Hornocker, M. G. 1967. "An analysis of mountain lion predation upon mule deer and elk in the Idaho Primitive Area." Ph.D. Thesis, Univ. of British Columbia.

old elk and mule deer than animals in their prime. These of course were the easiest to catch.

The next point to be considered is one of absorbing interest. What are the colours of a panther? The vast majority of reports tell of an animal ranging in colour from very dark brown through reddish to greyish, which are the normal colours of the cougar of the west, but there is a persistent minority of reports in the east of black specimens. I have eliminated all reports of black individuals seen at night, because all dark animals seem black after dark. There remains, however, reports like, "Jet black all over. It glittered in the sun, and its hide would make a beautiful pelt" (noted at 7:30 a.m.). "Jet black all over" was the observation of one who watched through a telescope for ten minutes. "Short shiny black hair on its body and tail" came from Nova Scotia, and "quite definitely black" was reported at 3 p.m. in New Brunswick. "Black as midnight" was noted at Fredericton in 1970.

No black panther or cougar has ever been killed in North America, but a sooty or slate-grey specimen from Florida was exhibited in the American Museum of National History. However, a black specimen has been shot in South America. It is described as follows: "The whole head, back and sides, and even the tail were glossy black, while the throat, belly, and inner surfaces of the legs were shaded off to a stone gray." I have puzzled over these reports for a long time. We must here make another decision. Either we accept the fact that there are rare black individuals to be found in the east, or we explain these apparently reliable reports in some other way.

My first thought was that these were specimens that had been backlighted. However, when the position of the sun, the animal and the observer are examined in these reports this explanation becomes untenable.

My next try to explain the black specimens was by assuming they were wet. A moose is brown when dry and black when wet. I went to Vancouver Island and hunted with the government cougar hunter until he killed a large male cougar. I took its fresh skin and propped up the edges and filled it with water and left it overnight. The next morning I observed and photographed it in colour from various distances and angles. I could not make it look black. When the purpose of this experiment was explained to the hunter he summed it up very well.

"I have hunted all my life in this bush and I have killed many cougars. I have never yet seen a dry one at the end of the chase, and I have never yet seen a black one either."

This leaves me with no alternative but to accept the eyewitness accounts at face value. I now believe there are a few black specimens of the panther in eastern North America. There were two in the Base Gagetown area of New Brunswick in 1955, and at least one in 1961. Another is reported in the same general area in 1967, and another was seen on the outskirts of Fredericton in 1970.

Between 1951 and 1970 I have collected twenty reports of black specimens which appear dry when seen at close range in daylight. Two were watched through rifle 'scopes, one for ten minutes. This evidence cannot be disregarded.

There is another long-shot explanation to which I give little credence: that the black individuals are escapees. We now know that lions can survive Canadian winters with a minimum of shelter. Why not leopards who live farther north in the Old World? Perhaps black leopards escaped, or were turned loose in this area, but none have been reported to the authorities.

The extreme northeastern section of the panther population has been almost isolated for more than 100 years, and it is in this section where melanism is most frequently reported. Black leopards have long been known from the tropical rain forests of southeast Asia. More recently they were found in the high wet forests of the Aberdare mountains in Kenya, where black servals are now reported.

However, if melanism were associated with a dense wet habitat we should expect to find it in the Pacific northwest, perhaps above all on Vancouver Island, where the animals are as numerous as anywhere else in North America. Yet a professional hunter who has killed many cougars there has never seen or heard of it. New Brunswick has far less rainfall than coastal British Columbia and the forest is not noticeably denser, so melanism is not apparently associated with dense wet forests on this continent.

If it has developed in this region as the records indicate, it is an extreme variation that has occurred in an isolated pereferal population, just as gigantism may be a trait that might have developed in another pereferal population in Patagonia. Black panthers have been reported annually from Florida where they are not hunted, so there is little chance of getting a specimen. This is yet another pereferal population.

In the 1700's and early 1800's a panther skin suit was a status symbol among the pioneers of eastern North America. This fad knocked the panther population of the east down to where the animal was finally called extinct. Today the fad has gone full cycle, and a coat of any of the striped or spotted cats is a status symbol among the wealthy. Again it is threatening the very existence of some species, as the prices men are prepared to pay make poaching rampant even in the countries where there are laws to protect them. The panthers' greatest protection today is that they are fortunate in only having spots when they are very young. If they were spotted throughout life they would be in great demand in the skin trade.

No description of the panther would be complete without a discussion of the various sounds attributed to it.

When the female comes into the heat she begins to call, and the male responds. This calling has been found in captivity to be carried on at intervals for many hours. One of the mysteries surrounding this animal is that in some areas (Idaho for example where lions are relatively numerous) this calling is almost never heard. In five years Hornocker never heard it. I once stood for four hours outside the cage of a female in a zoo while she called to her mate who was deliberately separated from her across the corridor. He made no reply, but she sat back on her haunches, threw back her head, opened her mouth to a full gape and uttered a call that began with loud catlike meows. It built up to a high, rasping, continuous scream, which lasted ten to fifteen seconds. It was an ideal opportunity to compare this call with the utterances of other large felines housed in the building. The female panther is well-described as the lyric soprano of the great cats. This cry has been recorded and is sold commercially as a hunting aid today.

Other sounds uttered by panthers have varied from soft, bird-like whistles, to a roar like an African lion but with less volume, repeated as a single "arouff" every few seconds. At the other extreme, a Nova Scotian described the sound made by a panther as "a noise twenty mad women could not make." But a call heard in Somerset County, Maine, where a panther track was found the next morning, was described by Wendell Taber like this: "I listened for quite some time in the middle of the night to what seemed to me an almost melodious series of loud continuous calls covering quite a range of pitch. Being acquainted with most sounds of the Maine forest night life, I was puzzled. I tried to associate the sound with some member of the cat family, but there seemed to be no association that I could distinguish. The following morning I found in mud, perhaps 200 yards distant, one footprint of a large mammal, a footprint as large or larger than that of a moose. This print matched perfectly the drawing Ralph S. Palmer supplied in his Mammal Guide for the Mountain Lion or Panther, *Felis concolor*."

Colonel Tex Purvis, the outfitter of jaguar hunters in Mexico, reports a mountain lion following him as he packed out a deer, and mewing like a large house cat all the way. The jaguar comes readily to the "roars" made by a horsehair in a gourd, but so far this device has not called up a puma.

In the San Francisco Zoo I watched a pair of mountain lions just before feeding time. As their excitement mounted they both gave high, shrill, and slightly wheezy calls that sounded like "W-a-ah! A-o-w-a-h!" If the sound were heard without seeing the source it would have suggested a much smaller animal. It was repeated two or three times in succession.

Roderick Haig-Brown of Vancouver Island, British Columbia,

suggests that the whistle might be a female calling her cubs. He and a companion had trapped and shot two cubs, and they heard the mother whistle on the hill above. They tried unsuccessfully to call her up by whistling in reply.

A very odd cry was described by Keaton in 1940. He shot porcupines for an old starving mountain lion that came to his mining claim in Idaho in the middle of winter. "Invariably after eating he would open his wide mouth and rumble and gurgle his thanks . . . a strange sound like that of water running over rocks and tumbling into a hole."[8] One wonders if the animal were starving because it had porcupine quills in its throat.

It is seen, then, that the panther is as vocal as any other cat, and makes a wide variety of sounds. However, it is normally a silent creature that chooses not to draw attention to itself, unlike the African lion which sends coughing grunts over the plain each evening as it sets out to hunt. The calls of a panther seem to be mainly, but not entirely, connected with mating.

However, it must be remembered that there are other creatures to be heard in the night forests of the northeast, and that every loud and thrilling noise is not the scream of a panther. Young horned owls, screech owls and barn owls make a variety of sounds in the night, which have no doubt sometimes been mistaken for a panther. Yet despite these red herrings, the real thing has undoubtedly been heard on several occasions.

Dudley F. Perley describes a New Brunswick panther's cry when interrupted in the midst of a deer hunt thus: "The sounds of the cougar I saw may be described as a series of gasping coughs, coupled with a very strange noise such as might result in the crossing of a pheasant's cry with that of a hog's squeal; these cries only given at the beginning and end."

After twenty-five years of examining, photographing and making plaster casts of their tracks I would expect the eastern panther of New Brunswick to be a long-legged subspecies very much like the Florida panther but with longer hair. Most of the tracks are in the three-inch-size class. Only the mature males reach the four and a half inches and up common in the west. It is for this reason that panther tracks are so seldom reported in a region under

[8] Keaton, J. B. 1940. "Bolivar my cougar chum," *Outdoor Life*. December.

snow for five months of the year. The tracks of many younger individuals and females are the size of those of a big bobcat. The lynx, rarer in New Brunswick than the panther, leaves tracks larger than those of a small panther. Thus the tracks of all three cats in the province are much the same size, and it takes careful observation to tell them apart.

A seven-foot Florida specimen measured only two and seven-eighths inches across the forefoot. I have plaster casts of the tracks of a New Brunswick specimen that was observed making them. It was a small animal, about five feet overall. They measure only two and a quarter inches across the forefoot and two and one-eighth inches across the hind foot in mud.

Panthers inhabit all types of terrain, from the mountains to the lowland swamps, and in a few places they even wander to the sea beach. They are found thinly scattered from the edge of the deer range in the Laurentians to where they merge with the southern race in Georgia and Louisiana. They thus cover in token numbers at least most of their original range.

This, then is the animal. One of the best examples of evolutionary perfection to be found in the animal kingdom.

# Chapter 5
## Methods of field study

When you are at the summer cottage at the lake, or the ski lodge high in the hills in winter, you may find tracks on the beach or in the snow that puzzle you. How can you tell if they are those of a panther?

The panther's track is four-toed, as are those of the other wild cats and dogs. A bear has five toes that show in its tracks. This quickly eliminates the bear. The track of a large timber wolf and that of a full-grown panther may be the same size, but the wolf track shows the unretractile claws of a dog and the rectractile claws of a cat do not show in the tracks of the panther in ordinary walking.

Even when the cat extends its claws in slippery footing or when climbing a bank the marks are distinctive. The claws of a cat are sharp hooks that, when extended, curve through ninety degrees and extend straight down to a fine point. Those of a dog curve down at only a slight angle from the horizontal, and are worn and blunt from constant contact with the ground.

The stride of the panther walking is about eighteen inches, while that of the wolf is slightly less, about ten inches.

Having eliminated the bear and any of the dog family by the number of toes and the presence or absence and type of claw, we are now reduced to the three types of wild cats in northern North America, the genera *Felis* and *Lynx*. A large lynx and a small panther may make the same sized tracks. In a very clear medium such as fresh mud or a skiff of snow it may be seen that the panther has a three-lobed heel pad and the lynx does not. In snow the lynx's track will appear blurred by the furry pad, and the panther's will remain clear, having no fur under the foot to blur it.

However the best method of distinguishing between the tracks of *Felis* and *Lynx* is to find tail drag. Unmistakable tail drag confirms the track as that of a panther, as both lynxes and bobcats are short-tailed cats. However caution is needed here. Tail drag can easily be confused with foot drag which many animals make. Tail drag usually alternates from side to side of the tracks, while foot drag marks start directly from a print and lie directly in front of it. Tail drag in a big panther is a mark two feet long and three inches wide pressed firmly into the snow. Where the panther is descending a steep bank it may well be to one side of the footprints as the animal swings the long heavy tail to balance itself.

Another way to distinguish between the track of a big lynx and that of a small panther is by the weight of the animal. A panther is far heavier than a lynx and will sink deeper into the medium. I have never used this method in anything but snow: place your closed fist on the surface of the snow beside one of the tracks. Press down with a weight of about twenty pounds. If the resulting print is as deep as the track, it is a panther, as a lynx would not put this much weight on one foot.

However, a decision should never be reached from a single print or set of prints. Always examine as long a section of the trail of the animal as possible for additional clues. One such clue is the bed. If a snow trail has been followed and the place where the animal has lain-up for the day has been found, it can yield additional information. When a panther lies down in the snow it usually curls up to conserve body heat. The long tail is wrapped around it leaving a telltale mark in the snow.

Another and important clue to be watched for along the trail is the scrape. Members of the cat family in North America use these scrapes as territorial markers along their trails, and will visit their old scrapes and make new ones every time they go by. Any stranger will also scrape and leave its scent at these places.

Several points of valuable information can be learned from scrapes. The first is whether or not this is a fixed territorial marker visited each time the cat is in the neighbourhood. This can be told by the number of scrapes. If it is a long-used marking place, there will be a number of piles of debris scraped up within a short radius. If there is only one it probably indicates no particular significance to the area. Mark all scrapes by sticking short sticks upright in the piles. Then the next time you visit it you can tell at a glance if the owner, or some stranger, has been there in the interval by the presence of an unmarked scrape.

If the scrape is in snow where such details can be seen, the width of the paw marks of each individual stroke and the spread of all the strokes give an indication of the size of the maker.

My British Columbia hunter told me that he often is able to tell the direction the cougar is travelling from the scrape if it is on a trail. The animal makes the scrape heading in the direction it is travelling by raking toward it the material in the pile. When it leaves, after depositing its urine or feces, it steps forward and often one of the hind paw prints may be found in the depression in front of the pile. The depression therefore lies in the direction the animal is travelling from the pile.

If you are fortunate enough to find a fresh panther track and follow its trail it will eventually lead to a kill. If the prey is a deer the killing bite will be on the back of the neck or the base of the skull. If the killer is an adult panther the canine tooth holes will be two inches apart. The bobcats and lynxes, lacking the jaw power and weight to use the back of the neck bite and head twist to break the deer's neck, attack by leaping on the animal and riding it while biting into the throat to suffocate it and sever the jugular vein. Their canine teeth are only one inch apart at most. All wild dogs attack on the flanks and rear, and do not attack the throat until the deer is down.

Great care is necessary in diagnosing kills to distinguish between the marks left on the carcass by the primary predator and those left by subsequent scavengers. Panther kills in New Brunswick are scavenged by bobcats and lynxes; coyotes, foxes, and feral dogs; ravens, crows, grey and blue jays; fishers and weasels; and in spring, summer and fall by raccoons. It can be seen therefore that to be positive that any clues left on the prey were made by the primary predator it is almost necessary to beat the scavengers to it. This is not often possible, as the best way to find kills is by watching the scavengers. Also, many crippled deer die after the hunting season and are fed on by these scavengers all winter.

The use of dogs in locating kills is a practical method. Any sort of dog strong enough to stand field work will do. I found several with my English setters, when searching for woodcock nests.

The deductions that may be made from a careful examination of the tracks of a panther can be summarized as follows:

Table 1 — *Deductions from panther tracks*

| Deduction | Evidence |
| --- | --- |
| *Age of the panther* | |
| Youth | 1. Size small to full size (four and a half by four and a half inches). |
| | 2. Toes round, not cracked and well-tucked in to the heel pad. |
| | 3. Heel pad not cracked. |
| | 4. Tracks register (hind paw track falls on forepaw track). |
| Old age | 1. Size (four and a half by four and a half to five and three-quarter inches). |
| | 2. Toes oval, cracked, and splayed out from heel pad. |
| | 3. Heel pad cracked. |
| | 4. Tracks do not register (hind paws fall behind forepaws). |

| | |
|---|---|
| *The speed of travel* | When cantering or galloping hind paws strike the ground ahead of forepaws. The distance ahead indicates the speed of travel. |
| *The age of the track* | 1. Ridges between toes damp; fresh track.<br>2. General weathering of section of the trail.<br>3. Presence or absence of insect tracks over panther prints.<br>4. State of crushed vegetation.<br>5. State of loose snow crystals (frozen or unfrozen).<br>6. Presence or absence of dew crust in sand.<br>7. Direction of wind and position of snow particles.<br>All considered with regard to the weather of the previous several days. |
| *The best time of day for tracking* | The early morning, before the day's weather has had a chance to blur the signs. |
| *The best angle to see tracks* | Always look into the sun if possible. |
| *Are two animals travelling together?* | Find where the tracks cross. If A is over B, and later B is over A, the animals must be travelling together. |
| *Is one animal following the other?* | If wherever their tracks cross, A is always on top of B, A is following B. |

Dew falls most heavily in the last hours of darkness in most places. It is therefore a good indicator of the age of tracks made during the night or in the early morning. If dew has fallen in the track as well as on the ground around it, the track was obviously made during the night. If there is no dew in the track, but dew on the ground around it, it was made after sunup. In sandy soil dew in a track will form a slight crust by caking as

134

soon as it is exposed to the sun. This crust remains after the other visible evidence of dew has disappeared in the heat of the day. It can be touched with the finger and broken, and the edges of the break are visible. If there is no crust and the soft sand runs freely to the touch, the print was made after sunup. The sharpness of the vertical sides of the track is then the best indicator of age. In sandy soil the edges start to tumble in shortly after the track is made, and the degree of obliteration is the measure of the age of the track.

The age of tracks in soft, dry snow can sometimes be told from the direction of the wind. If the track is in a position exposed to the wind, the fine particles thrown up by the animal walking through the snow will lie on the downwind side. Thus if there has been a north wind blowing during the night the particles will fall on the south side if the track was made at that time. If the wind switched to west at daylight, the position of the particles will show that the track was made before the wind changed.

A dim track in dust or sand can be brought out in bright sunlight by throwing a shadow on it. The contours of the track produce darker areas of shade, and the outline becomes visible. We found this technique most useful when hunting for panther signs along the logging roads and trails of the Big Cypress Swamp in south Florida. The only dry areas for miles in that region may be the artificially-built-up right-of-ways of the logging roads, and, as in British Columbia, these provide ideal places to look for panther signs.

Other deductions may be made from scrapes and scats found when following a panther. These are summarized as follows:

Table 2 — *Deductions from scrapes and scats*

| Deduction | Evidence |
|---|---|
| *The sex of the panther* | Males scrape often and plainly. Females scrape seldom and lightly. A female with cubs sometimes makes a large mound. |
| *The direction of travel* | The animal is travelling in the direction the depression points from the pile at the scrape. |

| | |
|---|---|
| *Age of the scrape* | New scats black; old scats white. Strength of smell of urine. General weathering of the scrape. |
| *Species of last kill and whether it is first or subsequent meal from it* | Hair and bones in scats indicate species of the kill. Soft parts and much blood in scats indicate first meal. Bones and hard parts, later meals. |
| *Direction and distance to lying-up point* | Large evacuation nearest lying-up place. Subsequent evacuations progressively smaller. Lying-up place lies in the direction of the increasing size of evacuations — usually on a high point with a view below, and largest evacuation is closest to it. |
| *Size of the panther* | Length of stroke at the scrape indicates length of leg. Width of individual strokes indicates width of paw. Both indicate size of animal. |

It is safe to say that all of these deductions and the evidence to base them on will not be present at the same time. The tracker must use what he has before him and continually search for the evidence on which to base his next deduction. Skill is only developed with practice, but when it is developed a surprising amount of information about your shy neighbour at the cottage or the ski lodge can be accumulated, and this in a manner which in no way disturbs a very rare animal.

If the opportunity to predict a panther's movements ever presents itself, the possibilities for making a photographic record should be carefully investigated. Flash traps have been used successfully on Barro Colorado Island in Gatun Lake in the Canal Zone by Frank M. Chapman in 1927. He used ordinary trip-wires to release the shutter. At least two pumas were recorded in pictures on this six-square-mile island which is a far smaller range than that required on the British Columbia coast. This would be expected under the lush tropical conditions of Panama.

The next successful flash trapper of mountain lions was Tappan Gregory in 1938. He operated in the Carmen Mountains in

the State of Coahuila, Mexico. This was a large-scale, well-organized expedition, in which many cameras were set and catnip oil lure was used. The firing mechanism was a buried treadle with electrical contacts. Mountain lions were numerous enough in the area to leave numbers of scrapes, offering many trap sites. However the camera that took the first lion picture had been set for sixteen nights before it was fired. The report of this expedition, and that of Chapman, should be carefully perused by anybody undertaking to flash-trap a panther.

For many years trappers have noted that a cougar will never go over anything that it can go under. They have taken advantage of this trait in setting traps for the animal. A trail is blocked by a small log or tree across it, leaving sixteen-seventeen inches open below the obstruction. This is narrowed to about fourteen inches with brush, and the trap is set with the pan about half an inch below the surface, directly under the log. The ground around, and right up to the jaws of the trap, is covered with small twigs and leaves. The trap pan is the only clear space left, and the cougar puts his foot on it. The same principle can be used for a flash-trap treadle.

Down through the years many ways of making a panther show itself have been tried. Perhaps the most strenuous was that of Lewis Dorman of Center County, Pennsylvania. He followed a panther on foot for nearly two months before he brought it to bay. A live-crated lamb, the more vocal the better, has been used successfully in the southwest. In the east the prize for imagination must go to Noah Hallman, an old hunter who lived near the

Blue Mountain Amphitheater in northern Berks County, Pennsylvania. He had several trained panthers which he used to lure wild specimens out of the rough country at the headwaters of the Lehigh River. These he roped and dragged back to camp in triumph.

The use of trail hounds is the surest way to catch a panther. This technique has a literature all its own which I will not attempt to cover here. However there is one point that I have found glossed over, and it is very important. It is that no dog can tell whether it is following an animal or backtracking it. That is why hound owners always hold the dogs in check until they have found a track to identify the animal and to be sure they are following it and not running away from it. If it is the species they want, the dogs are then loosed to run it.

When the dogs are in check pay particular attention to any trail they show interest in that runs along a log. This at once eliminates a deer and narrows the number of possibilities.

Today the roping of a mountain lion treed by dogs is commonplace in the west. A refinement that has made it even easier, and does not require such rough handling of the animal, is the use of a dart gun and drugs. Tranquillizers have been used successfully to knock out the specimen, which then can be weighed, measured, tagged and released to yield valuable data on its movements if it is recaptured.

The most recent development in this field is the use of telemetry. A small sending device is attached to the animal, and its movements are plotted by a team using a receiver from the ground or air. This is of course an expensive procedure which must be highly organized for maximum results. However, it seems to be the most promising method so far developed of following the daily movements of the animals, and will add much to our knowledge.

In this chapter we have seen what can be accomplished by using the ancient skills of the tracker, and adding to them modern advances in technique such as the use of drugs and telemetry. When the great increase in mobility provided by helicopters and ski-doos is added to the lethal skills of men and dogs, the safety margin of the species is appreciably reduced. It is in the light of these advances that this book is being written.

# Chapter 6

# *Some sighting sequences and their interpretations*

The time has come now to go back to our first assumption, that a series of reports from the same region may refer to the same animal or family group. There is no reason why this should be so, except that if they are from different animals there must be a much larger panther population in the area than the evidence suggests.

If we make this assumption and assemble some of these reports in chronological order, some interesting patterns develop. An example of this is the reconstruction of the life of a yearling panther that was abandoned by its mother in the Nashwaaksis Valley of New Brunswick in 1953.

That it was deserted then is fairly certain. Two full-grown panthers crossed an open field in broad daylight at the head of the valley in early June. They passed close to a herd of sheep and were completely oblivious to them, and of the shouts of the farmer who followed down his fence abreast of them for some distance. Only mating animals behave in that way. The same month the Nashwaaksis panther (as we will call the yearling the female had abandoned to its own devices) made its first appearance by bungling a kill nine miles away. Like all panther cubs in areas of a not overabundant food supply, it had been quite willing to allow its mother to do the killing for food. She was strong and sure, and the yearling could expend its ferocity upon the dead carcasses of the raccoon, hare, porcupine and deer that she killed. Now, however, the pangs of hunger were growing within its stomach because nothing had fallen to its clumsy rushes for several days.

We have seen how it was driven off by the cattle in its attempt to kill a young calf. The young panther had learned its lesson.

Never again did it attempt to take one of the young of these great animals that seemed so languid in the fields behind the farms. Raccoons, porcupines, hares and grouse made up the main part of its diet, until it gained full size and strength, and managed, probably after many futile attempts, to kill its first deer.

The yearling disappeared after this encounter, until the shooting season opened in the fall. When it was next reported it had crossed the main Nashwaaksis and followed up the North Branch to its head and along the ridge to Hurlutt Settlement, a distance of about seven miles as the crow flies. It had apparently spent the summer on the ridges between the Keswick and the main Nashwaak River. On the 15th of October it was standing in the open field of one of the abandoned farms of Hurlutt Settlement, when a party of four grouse hunters surprised it. All four stared at the large brown animal with the long sinuous tail, as it stood watching them from fifty yards. Then with a series of long loping bounds it disappeared into the woods.

The next day was the one that made it famous. On October 16, 1953, it crossed the North Nashwaaksis Stream above Carleton Lake, during the night, and hunted along the back of the fields toward the crossroads school of Birdton. It was following the same route its parents had taken in June. At eight-thirty in the morning the children arrived at the Birdton school. They played in the yard until the panther appeared. What followed next we have already heard.

It hunted southeast after its stay at Birdton, and, as we have seen, the next report came from about five miles away when it was missed by a deer hunter at Royal Road West.

Almost a month afterward its track was found again in deep snow in the black spruce swamp, beside the little lake that is the head of the West Nashwaaksis Stream. This was the last seen of the yearling. It was heading north for the great area of unsettled country about the head of the Tay, the Nashwaak and the Miramichi.

A further interesting example of reconstructing a panther's movements from a combination of field-sign and eyewitness testimony is the following account.

We have seen how on August 17, 1961, Frank McIntyre of Lawrence Station, Charlotte County, New Brunswick, was walking on a woods road two miles northwest of the junction of

Routes #27 and #3 in Charlotte County. This is about fifty miles southwest of my home. Suddenly he was startled to see two large catlike animals step out on the road ahead of him. The larger one was light tan all over, about two feet high at the shoulders and weighed about 150 pounds. The smaller one appeared darker in colour, and was about the size of a redbone hound. Both had long tails.

The larger one turned and looked at him, but the smaller never glanced back. They walked away around a bend and out of sight, with no sign of fear. Mr. McIntyre has hunted and trapped bobcats for more than fifty years. He drove to St. Stephen and reported to the Forest Service that he had seen a pair of panthers. Dick Gray of the Forest Service accompanied him back to the scene and made plaster casts of the fore and hind paws of a full-grown panther. These casts are in the Northeastern Wildlife Station today.

The animals had apparently been in this area all summer, as on May 26 Dr. V. A. Ellis of the Health of Animals Branch at Fredericton had reported a panther crossing the road in front of his car, about ten miles from where the track casts were made in August.

Nine days after Mr. McIntyre's encounter, and thirty miles to the northeast, R. S. Myles of Moncton was playing ball near his cottage at Lake George. He was chasing the ball through some tall grass when a large animal jumped up ahead of him and ran into the woods with a long loping gait. It was a cat with a large head which had a flat pugnosed appearance, and it was two to three feet from the tip of its nose to its rump. The tail was long.

The foreparts were grey or tawny, and the hindparts and tail appeared dark brown, almost black. On several occasions before this the Myleses had heard a strange catlike call at night, which had reminded them of a baby crying, and once before Mrs. Myles had caught a glimpse of a large cat.

Five days later, and twenty miles to the northeast, at Doak Settlement, York County, Mrs. John Crawford and her sons Robert, thirteen, and Roy, fifteen, and their cousin David, twelve, were bicycling along the settlement road early in the morning. A large cat was sunning itself on the side of the road. It moved off to a game trail when they approached. It was about the size of a police dog and appeared black in colour, with a long tail. The boys went to the nearest telephone and reported it to the Fredericton police, who called me.

I went with the boys to the mouth of the game trail and we found a partial print on the roadside. It was unmistakably cat, and the size of a small panther. Following down the game trail we found two beds in the sphagnum moss of a spruce swamp. They were about four feet long by two feet wide, and one was slightly larger and deeper than the other. Two typical panther scrapes were within ten yards of the beds. I instructed the boys how to make a track registration point where the game trail came out on the road, and told them to check it regularly and call me if they found fresh tracks. But none were seen. The animals had moved on.

They had not moved very far, however. Two weeks later one of them made the appearance that put them into the big time as a news item. At about seven a.m. on September 13, 1961, Norman Cody of 4 Elmcroft Place, Fredericton, looked out his window overlooking the river flats below the city. He saw a strange animal about 200 feet behind his house. This was about 100 yards from my home.

His first reaction was: "The Wrights must have a new dog."

Then he noticed that it was quite unmistakably a cat; not a dog. It was two to two and a half feet from nose to rump, with a long tail that dragged on the ground. It appeared tawny and flecked with white in the early morning sun. It crouched down, appeared to be having a bowel movement, and remained in sight for some time.

Mr. Cody took his binoculars and examined the animal care-

142

fully, and then called his wife and children to come and look at a cougar. He went to his bookshelf and took out an animal book, turned to a picture of a cougar, and compared it with the animal, using his binoculars. It tallied in every respect. Later he made a sketch of it for me. The animal then moved off out of their sight, and the family went to breakfast. Only about an hour later after breakfast did he call me two doors away — and I was out of town! He had had an opportunity to observe the animal over a period of time and examine it through binoculars. He compared it with the picture of a cougar in an animal book, and he is a professional artist.

My wife took the call and got in touch with my hunting partner, Dr. J. C. Likely. He and Harry Pridham examined the area some hours later and found some blurred tracks. In the meantime, the Fredericton *Daily Gleaner* had a team in the field, consisting of a girl photographer and a companion. They went through the dense tangle of the river bank calling: "Here Kitty! Kitty!" Some more tracks were found and photographed, but they were too indistinct to be useful. Nothing more was seen of the animal for two days.

Then on September 15, Sam Hubley was driving on Smythe Street Extension west of Fredericton at about 8 p.m. An animal that matched the description of the panther seen at Elmcroft Place two days before bounded across the road in his headlights. Its most prominent feature that stuck in his mind was the long, heavy, rope-like tail. It was heading down-river and away from town.

The rarest and least known of all our native animals had come within 100 yards of my home, and showed itself unconcernedly for some time to an appreciative audience. After twenty years of searching, the panther "anthered," but I was 200 miles away. Such are the frustrations of a wildlife biologist.

This series of events tells us that a litter of panther cubs may have been born in southwestern New Brunswick about a year and a half before. One was still with its mother as late as mid-August, 1961, and possibly to mid-September (the two beds found at Doak Settlement). The small size of the animal seen twice in Fredericton suggests that it was a half-grown cub. Whether it was less wary than its mother and was seen when she was not, or whether it was alone, we do not know.

The size indicated that the cubs were nearing the age of abandonment if they had not already reached it.

Thus may the movements of an animal or family group be reconstructed long after the event. This method requires an adequate reporting system to insure that the reports reach the record as soon as possible. It is the system used in India, together with tracings of pug marks, to keep track of the movements of tigers. It may be used as well for the study of elusive and rare animals in this country, especially as Canada has snow-tracking conditions for five months of the year.

# Chapter 7
## The future —
## status and research needs

When I first told Professor Aldo Leopold in 1947 that we still had a very few panthers surviving in New Brunswick, he was overjoyed, but fearful for their future. We decided to circulate the information only to selected organizations and individuals who might help in getting the New Brunswick government to pass protective legislation.

On May 5, 1947, he wrote me: "If this relic can be preserved I would not be surprised to see eastern states begging New Brunswick for breeding stock within the decade. Possibly reprints of the attached deer paper would help convince your administrators of the value of this remnant."

It appeared to be a simple thing to ask, and the proper authorities were approached. However, it was apparently naïve of us to expect results without pressure, and I was informed that no action would be taken on my request, as there was no demand for it.

The Dominion Minister of Lands and Mines in Ottawa then wrote on November 10, 1947: "In my opinion, full protection of the remnant of this species in New Brunswick is of great importance. Because of the scientific interest in the rediscovery of a supposed extinct race, New Brunswick holds a great responsibility to the remainder of eastern North America.

"I assure you that the National Parks Service will be happy to give full co-operation in preserving a limited population of eastern puma in New Brunswick."

This was powerful support, and we appreciated it.

The Curator of the Natural Science Department of the New Brunswick Museum then made an appeal. He was followed by the Provancher Society of Natural History of Canada from Quebec. Then came the Wildlife Management Institute of Washington, followed by the Nova Scotia Institute of Science. The Curator of Conservation of the American Museum of Natural History offered his help, and the Canadian Conservation Association added its voice.

The late Paul L. Errington, Research Professor at Iowa State College, suggested that the Wildlife Society should lend its support. He also urged that no specimens be taken for years to come. Taxonomic questions could wait.

Today the cougar of the west and the panther of the east exist in every province of Canada except Prince Edward Island and Newfoundland-Labrador, and the game administrators of the provinces know it. A very unique method of preserving this animal is used from Saskatchewan to the Atlantic. In this huge area no government will admit they exist. No one deliberately hunts them, so they are not directly endangered by man. His works, of course, destroy their habitat in one place and create it in another.

In British Columbia and Alberta the species is a game animal under management by the game management agency. This agency is free to close the season or open it, with the free flow of change in the population level of the animals and their environment. Provision for dealing with stock killers and other troublesome animals is simple. They are not bound by any special law which puts the species beyond the reach of good game management.

From Saskatchewan east this is not so. The animals have no status whatsoever. No Game Act specifically mentions them as a rare species that is protected, and it would be very difficult to make a case that would stand up in court against a man who kills one. The presumption that all animals not specifically mentioned in the Game Act are protected is wishful thinking on the part of the Game Departments. To commit a felony you have to do something that is prohibited specifically. Shooting a panther is nowhere prohibited. The killing of a lactating female would doom an entire litter, and as there may not be another female of breeding age in the area for many years, it would probably cause the surviving male to vacate the area entirely.

Today the only management possible from Saskatchewan to the sea is complete protection. But this may not always be so.

146

Conditions change and deer populations ebb and flow, and with them go the panthers. The game management agency must be free to act in the best interests of the animals and the people of the area, without hindrance from any special laws forced through by emotionally-motivated pressure groups. The species will require management, which may or may not mean complete protection in eastern North America from the present on. This means that the existence of the species must be recognized and it must be named in the wildlife laws of each province or state, and its status stated. It is not good enough to just ignore the animals any longer.

But since those days of twenty years ago we know that the panthers are not confined to New Brunswick. Rather, the whole of that part of the continent lying east of the Mississippi, between Florida and the Laurentians, is involved. In this region is the greatest concentration of people on the continent. The area therefore offers the maximum opportunity of seeing panthers. A sampling of how these rare and shy animals have been seen has been given in this book. But so far we have only counted the living. Let us now count the dead and wounded.

The old saw "If no more are killed in the next fifty years than were killed in the last, the species is in no danger" is badly in need of revision. This is the "locking the door after the horse is stolen" philosophy, with a vengeance. I have made a search of the records from 1900-68 for panthers killed or injured by man east of the Mississippi River and north of Florida. This list shows forty-five panthers killed or injured — a crippling loss of one every one and a half years, and very few of these were deliberately hunted. With the massive build-up of human population presently underway in this region, this rate may be expected to increase.

Fortunately, as we have seen, the animal is among the most versatile of all large mammals and can live in close proximity to man for some time without its presence being suspected. A few years ago a mountain lion lived for a period on a ridge that ran through a university campus in California. Its presence was a well-kept secret of the Department of Zoology until it moved on.

Animals that are dangerous to man, or harm his interests in any way, are always the first to be studied, if only as an aid to their extermination. It is a measure of the harmlessness of the panther that in all of these years almost nothing is known about

it from actual observation. It has never been photographed alive in the northeast.

The total number surviving in eastern North America, exclusive of Florida, may not be more than 100, and may well be less. We have all followed the long struggle to save the whooping crane. We have seen Canada put aside over 3,000 square miles as an inviolate sanctuary closed to all travel, even by air, for about fifty cranes to nest in. We have seen the United States Air Force asked to move its bombing range so that the cranes' winter home would not be disturbed. We have seen a strict sanctuary set up for the few remaining California condors to nest in, and we have seen what protection has done for the North Pacific sea otters. All of this is heartwarming and shows that, after a very slow start, we can be trusted to preserve endangered species.

But while we are taking this bow we must remember that the eastern panther is still inadequately protected, if at all, in every state or province in its range, except New Hampshire and Florida. A killing rate of one every one and a half years is not high, but on the other hand not many whooping cranes are being shot today. Not many Florida crocodiles or Key deer, grizzly bears or trumpeter swans, ivory-billed woodpeckers or Attwater's prairie chickens, California condors or sea otters are being killed. They are all endangered species, and are protected by law. The list is long, and the eastern panther is not on it except in the State of New Hampshire and that of Florida.

Florida, a major cattle-producing state and acutely conscious of the value of its wildlife, has pointed the way. Many cattlemen would have reservations about declaring a potential cattle-killer a protected animal. However, the Florida panther was disappearing fast and some form of protection was obviously needed if the animal was to be saved. The first step was to make it a game animal that could be hunted only under licence in the open season, and the season limit was set at one per year. Provision was also made for removing panthers which were damaging personal property at any time.

A few seasons showed that this could be done with no loss of panthers, simply because nobody hunted them. The open season was a sop to that portion of the human population that protest protection of any predator on principle. Then, after a few seasons, and with no complaints, a resolution of the Game and Freshwater Fish Commission was passed, on the Director's recommendation, that the panther be given complete protection as an endangered species — and so it is today.

We have here an extremely adaptable and tenacious species that has long been thought to have been extinct. We now find that it has survived drastic changes in its environment, is holding its own at a bare subsistence level, and has followed its prey into new territory. This has been possible solely because of an increase in the food supply. It has apparently passed the immediate danger of extinction, but in so doing it is coming more and more in contact with man. No other large wild animal has been able to do this in the settled portions of this continent without help from man himself.

Fortunately for the species, an increasing army of nature enthusiasts hunt only with camera and binoculars today. In some of the western states, Utah particularly, sportsmen appreciate the recreational value of the mountain lion. Instead of shooting the treed cat at the end of an exciting chase, they photograph it and let it go for another day. Herein lies the salvation of the species, and is the only type of panther hunting that should be tolerated in the east.

Other western lion hunters have undertaken private restocking projects by roping mountain lions and transporting them to ranges where the animal has previously been killed off. This not only provides more hunting opportunity, but helps prevent over-browsing by deer on overpopulated ranges. However it should only be done by professionals.

Gradually across the land the animal is receiving a better appreciation of its value. But bounties are still paid in South Dakota and in Texas. The bounty laws were repealed in British Columbia and Washington, and the state bounty was repealed in Oregon in 1961. But as late as 1967, seven Oregon counties were still offering a bounty. However, these were terminated that year and a one-year closed season was declared. Montana repealed the state bounty in 1962, and California in 1963.

In Oregon 201 cougars were killed in 1949, and only twenty-seven in 1961. The Legislature quickly dropped the $50 bounty on a species declining at this rate. Access and logging roads cutting into the last remote and primitive areas of the state have left few areas where cougars can remain secure from hound hunters.

Colorado was the first state to make the cougar a game animal. Under this new law the animal should hold its own in this state.

In Washington the cougar is a game animal with a bag limit of one per year. The extensive use of snowmobiles now makes it possible for hunters to cover hundreds of miles in searching for tracks in this country, and the animals are disappearing fast.

In Idaho the species was taken off the bounty list with surprisingly little opposition, and it is hoped that it will have complete protection, except for perhaps one per year or a special season, within five years. In 1971 a move was made to declare it a game animal.

In California the animal is only hunted for sport since the bounty has been removed, and there are probably not more than 100 hunters in the state who are willing to make the effort. Thus no great menace to the surviving lion population is apparent today.

In Nevada the cougar was given game animal status in May 1965. This requires a licence to hunt it, and there are restrictions on the kind of weapons that may be used.

In Utah it is also a game animal.

A most important announcement was made by the Boone and Crockett Club effective July 1, 1966. After this date "No cougar taken in any state, province or country which provides a bounty for taking cougar will be eligible for entry into the Boone and Crockett Club Big Game Competitions."

In 1966 British Columbia declared wolves, cougars and coyotes big game animals to be hunted only in season.

In 1971 Arizona moved to give the species game animal status.

In the east New Hampshire and Florida now give the animal complete protection, and the Florida panther and the survivors in southern Alabama and Georgia enjoy the added protection of the Endangered Species Act.

Thus at long last, a better appreciation of the relation of panthers and cougars to their prey is being expressed in North America. It is now more generally understood that the availability of the prey controls the number of predators, and that predator numbers do not control the prey.

What is needed now for proper management of the eastern panther is a clear statement of what we must know in order to plan management which will be meaningful. We must answer these questions. What is the present distribution of the animal? It is not good enough simply to say from the Laurentians to Florida and west to the gap in the deer range in Central Ontario. Specific localities must be recognized.

What is its population status? The best guess is that there are twenty-five to fifty maximum in New Brunswick alone. How many there are in Nova Scotia, Quebec and Ontario is completely unknown. The information from the eastern states is no better.

What is the breeding rate in the wild? Nothing is known about the panther in this respect in the north or the south. We must assume it is similar or very close to the western cougar.

What were the reasons for its original decline? The settlement of the country and the fact that a panther skin shirt was a status symbol among the pioneers were the initial causes. Heavy hunting and trapping pressure around the settlements resulted. The species is most fortunate today that it does not have stripes or spots when adult, or it would once again be in great demand as a status symbol among women whose husbands are in the higher income brackets.

What protective measures have already been taken and what more are needed? New Hampshire and Florida protect the species by law. The other states and provinces ignore its existence, as previously discussed. It should be made a game animal in all

151

states and provinces within its range, and no open season should be allowed until the numbers warrant it.

What further measures are available for management of the species? The possibilities for panther refuges should be considered. There the animal could be studied under wild conditions. The hills between the mouth of the St. John River and the mouth of the Petitcodiac River in Albert and Saint John counties in New Brunswick would seem to be a natural choice. Studies of the animal's habitat requirements, food habits, spacing and movements should be conducted by marking individuals, and by the use of telemetry. Areas should be located where females with cubs are seen. Zinc 65 as a feces tag planted in kills to yield data on local movements could be used experimentally.

There are no eastern panthers in captivity, but the southern subspecies breeds well in Florida zoos. An effort should be made to capture a pair for breeding purposes, if numbers ever rise to the level where this is possible. Care should be taken that they are not bred to other subspecies, and the local bloodline thus contaminated. Many fields of research that can only be pursued when captive specimens are available will then be opened. Breeding stock will thus become available for introduction in deer problem areas in the east.

A pilot experiment could be set up to study the relation of panthers to an overpopulation of white-tailed deer in an isolated habitat in eastern Canada. An ideal location would be on Anticosti Island, Quebec, where the deer have been introduced and there are no predators except man. Overbrowsing has altered the forest composition, and the deer have become "runty" despite heavy human hunting and poaching.

Such a project would need careful planning and execution, long after all necessary permission had been obtained. It would not be a simple matter of opening a cage door and turning loose a pair of zoo-bred panthers. They would have to be adults caught in the wild so that they would have learned to hunt and kill deer, and to be accustomed to living in a country with long winters and deep snow. The Gaspé Peninsula would probably be the best source of such stock if numbers there ever reached a level that would justify such a capture.

The greatest danger to the panthers today is from the "shoot it to prove I saw it" philosophy of most deer hunters. This, coupled with the ensuing panic which results from finding one-

152

self at close quarters with a large and desperately wounded cat fighting for its life, has so far discouraged any attempt at following up wounded animals. Especially is this true if there is failing light.

Is the steadily mounting number of deer hunters in the northeast, putting more and better equipped men into the woods each fall, of no significance? Is the ever-increasing miles of woods roads, carving into smaller and smaller chunks the remaining roadless areas where the panthers may feel secure, meaningless? And finally, are the endless miles of snowmobile tracks, crisscrossing the frozen lakes and seeking out the most inaccessible areas and making them available to anyone who can sit on a comfortable seat and be driven, of no consequence to the solitude-loving panthers? With the light plane overhead, and the radio-equipped snowmobile on the ground to aid the hounds, how much have the odds altered in favour of the hunter?

In the vast Idaho Primitive Area, a detailed study of the life history and ecology of the mountain lion was made. Lions were treed by dogs and immobilized with a dart gun and drugs so they could be examined, tagged and released. This yielded accurate measurements of their movements for the first time. Thus is reliable information gradually accumulating.

Florida and New Hampshire have broken the ice and led the way. How long will it be before other states and provinces in

153

the east follow suit? What does the future hold for the great tawny cats that look down from their high ledges at the ever-increasing works of man? I believe it holds survival, as there are still very many square miles where the deer step daintily along the lake shores. The panthers have shown us that everything they require for survival is at hand. All they need is man's permission to remain members of the club.

There is a growing body of naturalists and hunters who think the panther has a place in the wildlife scene of North America, and is a magnificent game animal in its own right, infinitely more difficult to hunt than any ungulate. However, experience has shown that no large mammal has survived in the east without the help of man in some form of protection. There is little reason to believe the panther will be the exception.

This book has attempted to dispel some of the fog of ignorance surrounding this rare creature whose mere name has closed schools and turned 700 hunters complete with mobile Red Cross Units and volunteer air patrols to vie for a $300 reward for killing it. If it has taken one step toward lessening this mass hysteria and developing a more enlightened attitude it will be a contribution.

Loss of this remnant now would be unworthy of a civilized society. We have been given a second and last chance. Let us make the best of it.

The International Union for Conservation of Nature and Natural Resources in Switzerland issues a Main List of the World's Rare and Endangered Mammals. The issue of April 1966 lists among them *Carnivora: Felis concolor couguar,* Kerr, 1792, the eastern panther; and *F. c. coryi* Bangs, 1896, the Florida panther. Florida has taken the necessary steps. How long will it be before others follow suit?

*"There is no such thing as a good or bad species. A species may get out of hand, but to terminate its membership in the land by human fiat is the last word in anthropomorphic arrogance."*

Aldo Leopold

# APPENDIX I.  SELECTED PANTHER REPORTS FROM EASTERN CANADA

| Date | Observer | Details |
|------|----------|---------|

**NEW BRUNSWICK**

THE SOUTHWEST RANGE

| Date | Observer | Details |
|------|----------|---------|
| Sept. 1920 | Charles T. Raynes | Sitting on boulder |
| Sept. 1934 | W. J. O'Brien | Met on the trail |
| 1938 | Forest Service Inspector, Earl Matheson | Fired at panther and missed |
| 1938 | Rural mail driver | Tracks and two sightings |
| July 1942 | Three men | Seen beside a lake by three men |
| June 1944 | Nixon | Catching frogs (See text) |
| Dec. 1944 | Man and child | Frightened skaters (See text) |
| July 1945 | Four men | (See text) |
| 1946 | Man on snowshoes | Panther seen on lake |
| Feb. 1948 | Joe Beck & wife | Two panthers crossed their farm (See text) |
| May & June 1948 | Man drinking from brook | Panther jumped on him (See text) |
| Dec. 22, 1948 | Winford Webb | Jumped an 8-foot fence (See text) |
| June 1950 | Forest Warden | Saw panther on road |
| Aug. 1950 | Two men | Swimming a river (See text) |
| Aug. 1953 | Bank of Nova Scotia manager & son | Watching model plane (See text) |
| Sept. 1953 | Driver | On road |
| June 1954 | Drivers | Three crossed road |
| Oct. 1955 | Charles T. Raynes | On hillside |
| Oct. 1955 | Hugh Purdy | Panther shot and lost (See text) |
| Oct. 20, 1957 | Dr. J. C. Likely & Dr. Torrie | Crossed the road |
| Feb. 18, 1958 | Fred Weeks & wife | Female in heat (See text) |
| 1961 | Driver | Following two deer |
| Feb. 1961 | Lady driver | Crossed the road |
| March 1961 | J. D. McDonald | Black specimen (See text) |
| Aug. 17, 1961 | Frank McIntyre | Female and cub (See text) |
| Oct. 15, 1962 | Two soldiers | A pair (See text) |
| Spring, 1963 | L. R. De Mond | On road |
| June 28, 1963 | Mrs. D. J. Scarratt & Miss Sue Corey | On road (See text) |
| July 5, 1963 | Dr. D. J. Scarratt | On road (See text) |
| Aug. 27, 1963 | C. Gordon Noble | (See text) |
| Oct. 11, 1965 | Driver | On road |
| June 21, 1970 | Driver | Crossed road |

THE WESTERN RANGE

| Date | Observer | Details |
|------|----------|---------|
| 1841 | Adams | Man reported injured near Fredericton by panther (See text) |
| 1900 | Forest Ranger report | Panther trapped (See text) |
| @ April 1904 | Two men | Panther comes to call of men. (See text) |
| Fall, 1920 | Edward Pugh | Panthers calling (See text) |
| Oct. 1940 | Walter Sangster | On road |
| 1940-1 | Trapper | Panther used the same circuit for 18 months. |
| March 1, 1941 | Teamster | Panther sitting in road (See text) |
| Fall, 1942 | Lone man | On road |
| 1944 | Driver | Fired at on road (See text) |

155

| Date | Observer | Details |
|---|---|---|
| Sept. 1946 | Sandy McArthur | Female surpristd at kill and fired at (See text) |
| Fall, 1947 | Trapper | Female with two cubs |
| April 1948 | ———— | Panther calling |
| June 1949 | Lone man | On road |
| May or June, 1948 | Ephraim Michaud | Panther attacks man. (See text) |
| July 23, 1951 | Driver | An immature panther crossed road. |
| Aug. 1951 | Hazen T. Gorman | Fired at and missed  (See text) |
| July 15, 1955 | Man & wife | Panther at 5 feet (See text) |
| Aug. 1955 | Driver | Crossed the road |
| Summer, 1957 | M. I. Kinney | Family group on road (See text) |
| March 1959 | Const. D. L. Lynch, R.C.M.P. | Report to C.O. "J" Division, R.C.M.P. (See text) |
| Oct. 1959 | Driver | Black specimen (See text) |
| Oct. 29, 1960 | Two men | Black specimen (See text) |
| July 1961 | A woman | Specimen of mixed colours (See text) |
| Aug. 26, 1961 | Her husband | Same animal (See text) |
| Aug. 31, 1961 | Three boys | Black specimen (See text) |
| 1962 | ———— | Seen near Fredericton |
| Sept. 11, 1963 | Steven Oliver | Crossed the road |
| Oct. 15, 1963 | Deer hunter | Fired at and missed (See text) |
| Nov. 1, 1963 | Fish Warden | Large male |
| Oct. 20, 1964 | M. McDonald | Panther sitting in a field (See text) |
| Sept. 16, 1966 | Walter Sangster | A full-grown adult (See text) |
| Sept. 28, 1966 | B. S. Wright | Crossed the road (See text) |
| Sept. 1966 | Mrs. Ruth Cleghorn | Squirrel kill (See text) |
| Nov. 20, 1966 | Driver | Crosses the road |
| Aug. 16, 1967 | Victor Collett | Black specimen (See text) |
| Aug. 18, 1967 | Man in a camp | Black specimen (See text) |
| 1968 | Drivers | Two specimens seen |
| April 12, 1970 | Two men | Black specimen (See text) |

THE BASE GAGETOWN
RANGE

| Date | Observer | Details |
|---|---|---|
| 1937 | Deer hunter | Fired at panther and missed (See text) |
| Aug. 1951 | Mrs. Harry Driscoll | Seen and heard calling |
| Fall, 1953 | Deer hunter | Panther missed (See text) |
| Fall, 1953 | Deer hunter | Panther wounded (See text) |
| May 1954 | Two people in a car | Saw panther crossing a field and tried to photograph it (See text) |
| Aug. 12, 1954 | Rural mail carrier | Four panthers (See text) |
| Sept. 1955 | Lt.-Col. Freeman Waugh | Black panther (See text) |
| May 1956 | Two soldiers | Saw panther on side of road |
| June 17, 1956 | Driver | Female with one cub (See text) |
| Oct. 1958 | Driver | Shaggy specimen (See text) |
| Oct. 1958 | Deer hunter | Watched with glasses (See text) |
| Jan. 1959 | Driver | Long-tailed "wildcat" sitting on snowbank (See text) |
| Feb. 1959 | Driver | Had to stop to avoid it (See text) |
| Sept.-Oct. 1961 | Three separate men | Young animal |
| Nov. 1961 | Cpl. C. F. Boyd | Black specimen (See text) |
| May 26, 1962 | Two Sergeants from Base Gagetown | Medium-sized specimen |
| June 14, 1962 | Driver | "Young tiger" |

| Date | Observer | Details |
|------|----------|---------|
| June 15, 1962 | Fredericton Police | Black specimen (See text) |
| 1962 | Cpl. Blair Hare | Black specimen (See text) |
| Fall, 1962 | Cpl. Blair Hare | Second-larger black specimen (See text) |
| Fall, 1962 | Two women | Panther running across field. Track cast (See text) |
| Winter, 1962 | Lt. Devaney, R.H.C. | Bed in snow (See text) |
| 1967 | Driver | Pass at 10 feet on road |
| 1969 | Soldiers | Three reports |
| July 8, 1969 | Indian Reservation | Pig kill (See text) |
| Aug. 15, 1969 | William de Lucry | Crossing road |
| Sept. 19, 1969 | Lt. Bondurant and Cpl. Sanford | Crossing road |

THE CENTRAL RANGE

| Date | Observer | Details |
|------|----------|---------|
| Fall, 1904 | John Gullison | Cub trapped (See text) |
| 1910 | Trapper | Adult trapped (See text) |
| 1918 | Lumber foreman | Panther sunning on boulder |
| 1932 | Deer hunter | Watched chasing deer (See text) |
| Aug. 1940 | Guy H. Hanson | Crossing a road |
| Spring, 1941 | ——— | Tracks reported for 6-8 years |
| Spring, 1943 | H. B. Allen | Seen by truck full of men |
| 1943-7 | ——— | Panthers seen |
| 1947 | Donald G. Currie | Panther driven off calf by cow (See text) |
| Nov. 2, 1947 | ——— | Several sightings |
| Jan. 27, 1948 | Farmer | Panther watched trying to cross the St. John River (See text) |
| July 1948 | Dr. D. B. Butterwick | Very dark specimen (See text) |
| Fall, 1948 | Deer hunters | Panther fired at and missed |
| Oct. 29, 1948 | Gerald Chute & Arley Marr | Called up a panther (See text) |
| July 1949 | Survey party | Panther estimated at 200 pounds (See text) |
| Aug. 1949 | R.C.M.P. | Following a deer trail |
| Nov. 1949 | A. W. O'Donnell | Panther fired at and missed (See text) |
| Early summer, 1952 | Bruce Duplessis | Panther with four cubs (See text) |
| 1953 | Donald Currie | Panther attacks and injures calf (See text) |
| 1953 | Farmer | A pair of panthers cross his field (See text) |
| Fall, 1953 | Bruce Duplessis | Panther eating chicken offal, shot and knocked down (See text) |
| Sept. 1953 | ——— | Two sightings |
| Oct. 15, 1953 | Four grouse hunters | Panther in an open field |
| Oct. 16, 1953 | Shirley White | Panther frightens children (See text) |
| Nov. 24, 1953 | Deer hunter | Panther fired at and missed (See text) |
| Spring, 1954 | Driver | Panther carrying a young ruffed grouse (See text) |
| Jan. 6, 1955 | Game Warden | Followed panther and watched making trail drag (See text) |
| Jan. 8, 1955 | Driver | Panther wounded in the foot (See text) |

| Date | Observer | Details |
| --- | --- | --- |
| Summer, 1955 | Drivers | Several sightings |
| Fall, 1955 | Deer hunters | Two adults and two cubs fired at and missed (See text) |
| Fall, 1955 | Deer hunters | Track $5\frac{3}{4}$ inches measured (See text) |
| July 28, 1958 | Farmer | Panther screeches at him from tree |
| July 5-Oct. 20, 1959 | A number of observers | Black panther. One fired at and presumably missed (See text) |
| Dec. 1959 | Hound hunter | Panther followed for 25 miles (See text) |
| April 1962 | Driver | Crossing the road |
| May 13, 1962 | Man & wife | Panthers at 53 yards through binoculars |
| June 1962 | A number of observers | Through binoculars at 75 yards. Black specimen |
| Nov. 26, 1963 | Two deer hunters | Panther digging in a field |
| May 1964 | Fisheries Officer | At 75 yards |
| Early summer, 1964 | Director of Mines | Crossing road |
| Sept. 1, 1964 | Lone man | He got up to within 50 yards on foot, before it ran (See text) |
| July 10, 1965 | Driver | Crossing road |
| Dec. 26, 1965 | Mrs. Thelma Cody | Panther fired at twice and missed (See text) |
| July 4, 1966 | Two men | Threw stones at panther at close range. I tried to call it up and may have succeeded. (See text) |
| Nov. 24, 1966 | Dr. J. W. Sears | Watched panther at 50 yards (See text) |
| 1967 | Driver | On road |
| June 1968 | Driver | Two panthers together |
| Aug. 2, 1970 | B. S. Wright & D. M. Trethewey | Black panther reported |

THE JUNIPER RANGE

| Date | Observer | Details |
| --- | --- | --- |
| May 1907 | Fred Hemphill | Panther calling |
| 1939 | Raymond Sweet | Panther watching grouse. Fired at and missed (See text) |
| July 1946 | A trout fisherman | Panther lying on log across stream (See text) |
| Sept. 1946 | A bicyclist | Panther sleeping on dirt road (See text) |
| Spring, 1947 | Muskrat trapper | Panther on old road |
| Oct. 1947 | Deer hunter | Panther at close range |
| Late summer, 1948 | Three separate observers | Three sightings |
| March 1949 | Fred Grant | Panther broke out of snare (See text) |
| June 1953 | Gate attendant | Panther watched him paint his gate |
| ———— | Road Grader Operator | Crossed it on the road |
| 1954 | Mining men | Crossed the road |
| 1954 | Earl Paget | Panther following a rabbit by scent |
| July 15, 1955 | Farmer | Calling at three-minute intervals |
| Aug. 1955 | Farmer and two children | Panther lying in an oat field |
| Fall, 1956 | Two deer hunters | Panther using scratching tree |
| Dec. 3, 1956 | Mr. & Mrs. Fred Grant | Young panther sketched from life (See text) |
| March 1959 | Driver | On the Trans-Canada Highway |

| Date | Observer | Details |
|------|----------|---------|
| Aug. 3, 1960 | Driver | On the Plaster Rock-Renous High-way |
| 1966 | Mr. S. Gormley | Pair in a doorway with owner standing on the porch |
| 1967 | —— | Two sightings |
| 1969 | Hazen Careef | An adult seen when deer hunting |

THE NORTHWEST
RANGE

| | | |
|------|----------|---------|
| @ 1965 | Driver | Crossing road |

THE RESTIGOUCHE-
NIPISIGUIT RANGE

| | | |
|------|----------|---------|
| Aug. 1930 | J. G. Veness of the Dom. Forest Service | Met on the trail |
| 1938 | Fred J. Farrell | Panther seen moving in front of forest fire (See text) |
| 1938 | —— | Panther seen on Gouamitz River |
| 1948 | Two deer hunters | Shot at 2 panthers hunting together (See text) |
| Sept. 1951 | Driver | Black specimen (See text) |
| 1953 | Four guides | Panther on river bank (See text) |
| Aug. 1955 | Head, N.B. Soil Survey | On the road |
| Deer season, 1957 | Deer hunter | Large adult fired at and missed (See text) |
| 1959 | Survey party | Black specimen (See text) |
| July 10, 1960 | Two men, N.B. Forest Service | A half-grown cub |
| Feb. 1961 | Driver | Large adult crossed road |
| Summer, 1961 | Fisherman | Finds deer kill on gravel bar (See text) |
| Aug. 9, 1963 | Fire tower lookout | A large adult |
| Aug. 15, 1963 | Driver | On road |

THE MIRAMICHI
RANGE

| | | |
|------|----------|---------|
| 1900 | Dr. Wm. J. Long | Finds a panther's den and a caribou kill (See text) |
| Fall, 1908 | J. W. Fairley | Wounded and lost a panther (See text) |
| 1914 | Trapper | Reported tracks |
| Fall, 1919 | Two deer hunters | Fired at a running panther and missed |
| 1919-20 | Hunters | Tracks reported |
| 1919-20 | Forest Ranger P. W. Vanderbeck | One seen and 2 trapped (See text) |
| Sept. 16, 1922 | Edward Pugh | Panther jumped by deer drive |
| Nov. 1923 | Collingwood Fraser | Panther shot (See text) |
| Spring, 1926 | A fisherman | Panther on river bank |
| 1930 | J. G. Neill & survey party | A panther, tracks and calls seen and heard |
| Summer, 1931 | Dr. Arthur S. Chesley & party | Panther watched swimming river (See text) |
| 1939 | Two fishermen | Panther on portage road |
| Aug. 1940 | A local man | Panther at 30 yards |

| Date | Observer | Details |
|---|---|---|
| Fall, 1940 | Deer hunters | Fired at on several occasions and missed |
| Fall, 1947 | Two hunters | Panther at 26 feet (See text) |
| June 13, 1948 | Driver | Crossed the road |
| Sept. 29, 1948 | A fisherman | Panther watched him fish |
| Dec. 18, 1948 | Game Warden | Panther reported |
| Jan. 1949 | Hunters | Panther reported |
| Dec. 1950 | Two men in a truck | Panther at 50 feet |
| Nov. 1, 1952 | Deer hunter | Panther at 75 paces |
| 1954 | Farmer | Panther leaps into old cans and is frightened (See text) |
| June 19, 1955 | Two men | Crossed the road |
| Feb. 25, 1957 | Man & wife | Panther running across field (See text) |
| Summer, 1963 | Local people | Pair reported at intervals all summer (See text) |
| Oct. 1968 | Two hunters | Panther on Dungarvon River |

THE KENT-
WESTMORELAND
RANGE

| | | |
|---|---|---|
| Oct. 1919 | Land Surveyor | Panther at 30 yards (See text) |
| March 1932 | Havelock Robertson | Panther shot, skinned and photographed (See text) |
| Oct. 1947 | Game Warden, John Tingley | Saw panther at the N.S. border (See text) |
| Sept. 1957 | Man & wife | Panther swims river |
| Oct. 1958 | A fisherman | Panther at 53 yards |
| May 28, 1960 | Driver | Crossed the road |
| Oct. 1966 | Driver | Crossed the road |
| June 3, 1969 | Wildlife Park employee | Panther "shedding" |
| Aug. 11, 1971 | J. E. Hemphill & Raymond Cyr | Crossing Trans-Canada Highway |

THE SOUTHERN
RANGE

| | | |
|---|---|---|
| Oct. 1921 | Clairmont Dykeman | Shot, crippled and lost. Bone splinters recovered (See text) |
| 1923 | Mrs. Otho H. Bishop | Female with 2 cubs (See text) |
| Late summer, 1930 | Mrs. R. J. Johnson | Female with 3 cubs (See text) |
| Fall, 1939 | Forest Ranger | A number of deer kills |
| April 1944 | ———— | Panthers seen 3 times |
| March 1947 | B. S. Wright | Track photos taken of a family group (See text) |
| July 1947 | B. S. Wright | Plaster casts taken (See text) |
| ———— | ———— | Tracks of female and 1 young cub found (See text) |
| Nov. 1947 | Hunters | Two adults and 2 cubs seen together (See text) Two adults seen together. Fired at and missed (See text) |
| March 19, 1948 | Two men | Watched panther urinate on tree |
| May 1948 | Registered guide | Panther chases deer across road (See text) |
| Oct. 25, 1948 | Hunter | Panther wounded (See text) |

| Date | Observer | Details |
|---|---|---|
| Aug. 1950 | Driver and 3 passengers | Crossed the road |
| Oct. 1951 | Deer hunters | Saw panther on side of road |
| Nov. 22, 1951 | Herman Belyea | Panther chased man out of the woods (See text) |
| 1954 | Farmer | Panther crossing fields |
| Early spring, 1954 | Photographer | Attempted to take pictures of the panther lying on a log (See text) |
| Oct. 1, 1955 | Park Warden, Fundy National Park | Crossed road (See text) |
| Oct. 5, 1956 | Driver | Crossed road |
| Spring, 1957 | Local residents | Watched through binoculars for 10 minutes |
| Aug. 1957 | Driver & 5 passengers | Panther at 5 feet (See text) |
| Summer-fall, 1958 | Several people | A total of 7 sightings (See text) |
| 1958 | George Miller, ex-Chief Forester of N.B. | Crossed road (See text) |
| Feb. 1959 | Rural mailman | Black specimen |
| July 30, 1959 | Driver | Stood in the road and forced a car to stop |
| Sept. 12, 1959 | Fundy National Park | Very dark specimen |
| Oct. 16, 1960 | Deer hunter | Panther sat in road at 75 yards |
| March 1961 | A house owner | Panther sniffing around garbage barrel |
| April 6, 1962 | A couple | Panther frightened them by leaping from a tree |
| Summer, 1962 | Mrs. D. F. Reid | Frightened by black panther leaping toward her (See text) |
| Nov. 2, 1963 | Harold H. Prince, Wildlife Graduate Student | Panther fired at and missed (See text) |
| Nov. 1963 | Ernest T. Geldart | Panther fired at and wounded (See text) |
| June 8, 1970 | Four Park Naturalists | Panther crossed the road (See text) |
| Aug. 19, 1970 | Pearl & Connie Colpitts | Crossing road |
| Nov. 10, 1970 | Charles Shaw | Panther watching him when deer hunting |
| June 13, 1971 | D. B. Banks, Fishery Biologist | Crossing road |
| Sept. 29, 1971 | Minister of Justice & Mrs. J. B. M. Baxter | On lawn at 50 feet (See text) |

## NOVA SCOTIA

| Date | Observer | Details |
|---|---|---|
| June 1923 | Wife of a farmer | Chased their collie dog (See text) |
| 1941 | Driver & passenger | Had to stop to avoid a panther (See text) |
| 1944 | Four people | Panther shot with a BB gun (See text) |
| 1945-7 | ——— | Several reports |
| June 1948 | Lone man on foot | He climbed a tree to avoid it (See text) |
| Oct. 1948 | Man & wife | Panther at close range |
| Dec. 1949 | Ex-towerman on Blue Mountain Fire Tower | Saw panther near deer kill (See text) |
| 1951 | Driver | Female and 2 cubs (See text) |
| June 1952 | Driver | Crossing road |

| Date | Observer | Details |
|---|---|---|
| Aug. 1, 1952 | Fisherman | Panther lying on rock (See text) |
| Sept. 1, 1952 | Driver | Black specimen on roadside (See text) |
| Fall, 1952 | Driver | Runs over cub (See text) |
| 1953 | Driver | Crossing road. Possible calf kill (See text) |
| 1954 | Assistant Provincial Forester | Crossing road (See text) |
| 1954 | A number of observers | A number of reports |
| 1954 | Two fox hunters | Panther calling in tree (See text) |
| March 12, 1954 | L. A. Duncanson | Track casts made (See text) |
| Oct. 14, 1954 | Driver | Crossing the road |
| May 27, 1959 | Driver & 2 passengers | Panther in sight for half an hour (See text) |
| June 1959 | Man & 2 sons | Panther apparently interested in dead gaspereaux (See text) |
| Aug. 14, 1959 | Three trout fishermen | Panther on lakeshore watches fishermen (See text) |
| Nov. 1959 | Fisherman | Panther on lakeshore |
| March 1962 | H. A. Macdonald & 13 others | Pair of panthers frightens the village (See text) |
| March 19, 1963 | Chairman, Cougar Committee, Antigonish Fish & Game Association | Dog trees panther, but when man leaves to get gun it descends and kills dog |
| Feb. 27, 1964 | Forest Ranger & Pilot | Aerial moose count crew sees panther (See text) |
| March 1964 | Snowplough operator | Panther kills deer (See text) |
| June 1964 | Fishery Warden | Dog trees panther which escapes (See text) |

## QUEBEC
GASPÉ

| Date | Observer | Details |
|---|---|---|
| Mid-July, 1885 | Sir C. G. D. Roberts | Panther calling at night (See text) |
| Oct. 1951 | Claude Minguy, Wildlife Biologist | Panther and bear fight to the death (See text) |
| July 11, 1952 | Manager, Hammerville Paper Co., his wife, & another couple | Panther on the road |
| Summer, 1954 | Martin Bovey | On road (See text) |
| Oct. 10, 1957 | Arthur C. Dixon | On road |
| 1959 | Game Warden | On road |
| June 1961 | Director of Quebec Park Service & the Superintendent of Gaspé Park | On road |
| July 3, 1962 | Inspector, Quebec Park Service | Panther sunning itself |
| Nov. 8, 1963 | Biology student & friend | Female and cub |

SOUTHERN ZONE

| Date | Observer | Details |
|---|---|---|
| June 30, 1828 | E. Grieve | Specimen in the National Museum from Three Rivers (See text) |
| 1840 | ———— | In National Museum. Shot in a basement in Sherbrooke (See text) |

| Date | Observer | Details |
|------|----------|---------|
| 1847 | ——— | Shot on Croil's Island in the St. Lawrence. Parts now in the National Museum (See text) |
| 1859 | John Lemming | In Redpath Museum at McGill University (See text) |
| Oct. 3, 1863 | Jacques Gamelin | Panther drowned swimming Lake St. Peter (See text) |
| Nov. 21, 1909 | W. A. Learo, taxidermist | Panther shot on Mount Royal (See text) |
| 1919-20 | Dom. Bureau of Statistics | Eight panthers shot or trapped in Quebec (See text) |
| Jan. 1938 | Rosarie Morin | Trapped a panther (See text) |
| March 7, 1959-<br>April 18, 1959 | Izaak Hunter | Family of 3 seen on Montreal Island (See text) |

NORTHERN ZONE

| Date | Observer | Details |
|------|----------|---------|
| March 1880 | Thomas Anderson, H.B.C. | Panther shot by Indian (See text) |
| 1947 | ——— | Hawk Lake |
| 1955-8 | ——— | St. Maurice Valley |
| Nov. 2, 1958 | ——— | Mt. Tremblant Park |
| 1960 | ——— | Snow River |

# APPENDIX II. SELECTED PANTHER REPORTS FROM THE EASTERN UNITED STATES

| Date | Observer | Details |
|---|---|---|
| **MAINE** | | |
| May 1897 | Alfred Anderson | Panther feeding on a dead horse (See text) |
| Aug. 1900 | Fishermen | Panther on lakeshore |
| 1914 | Whole camp crew | Panther trying to steal a quarter of beef |
| 1915 | Fred J. Farrell | Shoots panther (See text) |
| 1924-5 | Driver | On road |
| June 1, 1929 | Fisherman | Panther swims brook |
| Aug. 5, 1943 | ———— | Panther reported |
| Aug. 2, 1943 | ———— | Panther follows man |
| Late summer, 1948 | Lady on a farm | Panther standing on its hind legs (See text) |
| Nov. 1949 or 1950 | Judge R. Weatherbee | Panther watching truck (See text) |
| Sept. 10, 1950 | Game Warden, Virgil E. Ladd | Panther fired at with pistol but missed (See text) |
| June 15, 1953 | Game Warden, Harold W. Green | Panther screeched at a woman in a field (See text) |
| Sept. 14, 1958 | White Nichols | Sketched five-toed track (See text) |
| Aug. 13, 1965 | Charles Wilcox | Five panther cubs on road (See text) |
| **NEW HAMPSHIRE** | | |
| Aug. 27, 1948 | Charles L. Robinson | Crossed the road |
| Aug. 29, 1948 | ———— | Crossed the road |
| Sept. 2, 1948 | Charles M. Saxe | A well-grown cub |
| Sept. 1948 | ———— | Panther watched picnic party cooking steaks (See text) |
| **VERMONT** | | |
| 1948 | Fire tower lookout | Report from short range |
| 1950 | Fire tower lookout | Report from short range |
| April 2, 1963 | Claxton Brown | Threw snowballs at a panther to make it move (See text) |
| **NEW YORK** | | |
| Aug. 1956 | George Crossette | Panther beside road |
| July 1961 | Man & wife | Crossed the road |
| Sept. 26, 1965 | Man & wife | Crossed the road |
| **MASSA-CHUSETTS** | | |
| 1953 | ———— | Several reports |
| Feb. 13, 1960 | Conservation Officer, Roland D. Gaudette | Followed tracks of 2 panthers (See text) |
| Nov. 15, 1960 | Harry N. Donaldson | Panther hit by car on the Mass. Turnpike (See text) |
| Oct. 12, 1968 | Jack Swedburg | Crossed road (See text) |
| Aug. 25, 1969 | Harry Hodgson | Panther on road (See text) |
| **NEW JERSEY** | | |
| Late May, 1958 | Dr. William V. Garner | Panther on turnpike |
| **CONNECTICUT** | | |
| 1967 | ———— | Two sightings |

| Date | Observer | Details |
|---|---|---|
| **MARYLAND** | | |
| 1971 | Fred J. Rosenbaum | Crossed the road |
| **PENNSYLVANIA** | | |
| Oct. 28, 1967 | John Gallant | Young panther shot (See text) |
| **WEST VIRGINIA** | | |
| 1936 | U.S. National Museum | Tracks identified (See text) |
| **THE CAROLINAS & GEORGIA** | | |
| | The work of Herbert Ravenel Sass | |
| 1948 | ——— | Manager of a plantation meets a panther at night (See text) |
| 1951 | ——— | Panther leaps on the roof of a house (See text) |
| 1951 | ——— | Several seen ahead of deer hounds |
| 1951 | ——— | Female and cub |
| 1952 | B. M. Badger | Found freshly-killed carcass on the road |
| Prior to 1954 | ——— | At least two panthers killed by cars (See text) |
| **ALABAMA** | | |
| March 16, 1948 | A. D. Hare | Panther shot and preserved (See text) |
| 1956 | Biology Dept. of Univ. of Alabama | Panther shot and preserved |
| 1962 | U.S. National Museum | Tracks identified |
| **MISSISSIPPI, LOUISIANA & ARKANSAS** | Panthers known to exist, but no effort has been made to collect reports | |

# PANTHER OBSERVATIONS USED IN THIS BOOK

**Eastern Canada**

New Brunswick

| | |
|---|---:|
| The Southwest Range | 32 |
| The Western Range | 38 |
| The Base Gagetown Range | 27 |
| The Central Range | 48 |
| The Juniper Range | 21 |
| The Northwest Range | 1 |
| The Restigouche-Nipisiguit Range | 14 |
| The Miramichi Range | 28 |
| The Kent-Westmoreland Range | 9 |
| The Southern Range | 37 |
| Total—New Brunswick | 255 |
| Nova Scotia | 26 |
| Quebec | 23 |
| Total—Eastern Canada | 304 |

United States

| | | |
|---|---:|---|
| Maine | 14 | |
| New Hampshire | 4 | |
| Vermont | 3 | |
| New York | 3 | |
| Massachusetts | 5 | |
| New Jersey | 1 | |
| Connecticut | 2 | |
| Maryland | 1 | |
| Pennsylvania | 1 | (many others) |
| West Virginia | 1 | |
| The Carolinas & Georgia | 6 | |
| Alabama | 3 | |
| Total—United States | 44 | |
| Total—Eastern North America | 348 | |

BIBLIOGRAPHY (based on the range of the eastern panther as shown by Young and Goldham 1946)

Adams, A. L. 1873. *Field and forest rambles with notes and observations on the natural history of eastern Canada.* London. Henry S. King and Co.

Allen, G. M. 1904. *Fauna of New England.* Occas. Papers. Bost. Soc. Nat. Hist. 7: 21.

Allen, G. M. 1942. *Extinct and vanishing mammals of the western hemisphere.* Spec. Publ. Amer. Committee for Intern. Wildlife Prot. 11 (Dec. 11). 620 pp.

Allen, J. A. 1869. *Catalogue of the Mammals of Massachusetts: with a critical revision of the species.* Mus. Comp. Zool. 8: 153. Cambridge.

Allen, J. A. 1876. "The former range of some New England carnivorous mammals," *Amer. Nat.* 10: 708-715.

Allison, E. 1962. "Killer of the Everglades," *Sports Afield.* Feb.

Ames, C. H. 1901. "Maine panthers again." *Forest & Stream.* 56(20); 385, May 18.

Anderson, R. M. 1937. "Fauna of Canada," *Canada Yearbook.* 29-52. Dominion Bureau of Statistics. Ottawa.

Anderson, R. M. 1938. "Mammals of the Province of Quebec," *Soc. Provancher d'Hist. Nat. Canada.* 50-114. Ottawa.

Anderson, R. M. 1947. *Catalogue of recent Canadian mammals.* Nat. Mus. Canada. Bull. No. 102.

Anonymous. 1850. Editorial—*Frontier Palladium.* Malone, New York. Aug. 1.

Anonymous. 1868. *Killing of panther.* Franklin. Franklin County, N.Y. Malone Palladium. Jan. 2.

Anonymous. 1878. "Adirondack panthers," *Forest & Stream.* 10: 138.

Anonymous. 1880. "Big game near Memphis, Tennessee." *Chicago Field.* 13(1): 11.

Anonymous. 1894. "The panther in Canada," *Biol. Review of Ontario.* 1(3): 49-50. July. Toronto.

Anonymous. 1931. *Animal Life* Zo (1): 37. Ont. SPCA, Toronto.

Anonymous. 1943. "Indiana fur value shown in invoice left by (Francis) Vigo of Vincennes three lifetimes ago," *Outdoor Indiana.* 10(10): 3. 15 Nov.

Anonymous. 1944. "These were former Pennsylvanians." Penna. *Game News.* 15(9): 21. Dec.

Audubon, J. J. and J. Bachman. 1851. *The viviparous quadrupeds of North America.* New York. Vol. 1: 256-257. Vol. 2: 305-313.

Backus, Wm. 1956. "Persistent reports bring us the mountain lion." N.J. *Outdoors.* 6(7): 12-13. Jan.

Bailey, V. 1933. "Cave life of Kentucky," *Amer. Midl. Nat.* 14(5): 47.

Baird, S. F. 1857. *General report of the North American mammals, including descriptions of all known species chiefly contained in the Museum.* Smithsonian Inst. J. B. Lippincott & Co. Phila. Pa. 85-86.

Baird, S. F. 1859. *Mammals of North America.* J. B. Lippincott & Co. Phila., Pa. 83-86. 764 pp. illus.

Bartram, Wm. 1928. *The travels of William Bartram.* Edition Mark Van Doran. Macy-Masius.

Beverly, R. 1705. *The history and present state of Virginia.* Four parts or books. English version.

Beverly, R. 1707. *Histoire de la Virginie.* Thomas Lambrail. Amsterdam. 433 pp.

167

Bider, J. Roger. 1968. "Animal activity in uncontrolled terrestrial communities as determined by a sand tracking technique. "Ecological Monograph 38. August. 269-308.

Boardman, G. A. 1899. "St. Croix mammals," *Calais Times*. Calais, Maine. Nov. 23 reprint. The Naturalist of the St. Croix, S. L. Boardman. Bangor 1903. 319-321.

Bole, B. P. Jr. and P. N. Moulthrop. 1942. "The Ohio recent mammal collection in the Cleveland Museum of Natural History." Cleve. Mus. Nat. Hist. Sci. Pub. 5(6): 83-182. Sept.

Brayton, A. W. 1882. *Report on the mammalia of Ohio*. Geol. Surv. of Ohio 4: 1-185.

Brimley, C. S. 1939. *Mammals of North Carolina*. North Carolina Dept. Agric., Div. Entomology. 2.

Brodie, Wm. 1894. "The panther in Ontario," *Biol. Review of Ontario*. 1(2): 27-28.

Brooks, F. E. 1910. *Mammals of West Virginia*. West Va. State Board of Agric. Report 20: 9-30. Quarter ending Dec. 20. Charleston.

Brooks, M. 1965. *The Appalachians*. Houghton Mifflin Co. Boston. Riverside Press, Cambridge.

Browning, M. 1928. *Forty years of the life of a hunter*. In Young, S. P. and E. A. Goldman. 1946.

Buffon, G. LL. de. 1776. *Histoire naturelle. Général et particulière. Servant de suite à l'histoire des animaux quadrupedes*. Supp. Vol. 3: 1-XXI, 1-330, 65 pls.

Burt, W. H. 1946. *The mammals of Michigan*. Univ. Michigan. Ann Arbor. 303 pp.

Butler, A. W. 1895. *A century of changes in the aspects of nature*. Proc. Indiana Acad. Sci. 31-40.

Cabrera, Angel. 1961. *Los felidos vivientes de la República Argentina*. Mus. Arg. Cience. Nat. Ciencias Zool. TVI. No. 5. Buenos Aires, 247 pp.

Cahalane, V. H. 1958. *Mammals of North America*. MacMillan. New York.

Cahalane, V. H. 1963. "The American Cats." Chap. 3 in *Wild Animals of North America*. M. B. Grosvenor Editor-in-Chief. Nat. Geo. Soc. Washington, D.C.

Cahalane, V. H. 1964. *A preliminary study of the distribution and numbers of cougar, grizzly bear and wolf in North America*. New York Zoological Soc. September.

Cahalane, V. H. 1965. "Cougars (*Felis concolor*) in the U.S. are barely holding their own," *Audubon Magazine*. May 67(2): 108-109.

Calcutt, J. 1894. "The American panther," *Biol. Rev. Ontario*. 1(2): 23-26. Toronto. April.

Cameron, A. W. 1956. *A guide to eastern Canadian mammals*. Nat. Mus. Canada. Ottawa.

Cameron, A. W. 1958. *Mammals of the islands in the Gulf of St. Lawrence*. Nat. Mus. Canada. Bull. #154. 156 pp. Biol. Series 53. Ottawa.

Carver, J. 1838. *Carver's travels in Wisconsin*. (A reprint of *Travels through the interior parts of North America in the years 1766, 1767, 1768*.) London. 1781. I-XXXII: 1-376. Map and illus.

Catesby, M. 1743. *The natural history of Carolina, Florida, and the Bahama Islands*. London. Vol. 2: XXV.

Cawthon, J. 1957. "The day the panther prowled," *West Vir. Cons.* 21(9): 12-13. Nov.

Chamberlain, M. 1884. *Mammals of New Brunswick.* Bull. Nat. Hist. Soc. N.B. 3(4). 37-40.

Chamberlain, M. 1892. *Mammals of New Brunswick.* Bull. Nat Hist. Soc. N.B. 10(2): 30-33.

Chapman, F. M. 1927. "Who treads our trails," *Nat. Geo. Mag.* Sept.

Chichester, B. 1943. "Cougar trails," *Rod and Gun in Canada.* 45(3): 12-13, 27. Illus. Montreal, Canada. August.

Clarke, C. H. D. 1969. "The Puma in Ontario," *Ontario Fish and Wildlife Review.* 8(4). Winter, 7-12.

Colvin, V. 1879. "Seventh annual report on the progress of the topographical survey of the Adirondack region of New York to the year 1879." Assembly Doc. 87: 159-160. March 7.

Connally, J. E. Jr. 1949. "The food habits and life history of the mountain lion, *Felis concolor hippolestes.*" Unpublished MSc thesis. Dept. of Vertebrate Zoology. Univ. of Utah.

Cooney, R. 1832. *A Compendious history of the northern part of the Province of New Brunswick and the District of Gaspé in Lower Canada.* Reprinted in 1896 by D. G. Smith at Chatham, Miramichi, New Brunswick, from one of the original copies printed by Joseph Howe. Halifax.

Cory, C. B. 1912. *The mammals of Illinois and Wisconsin.* Field Mus. Nat. Hist. 11: 153, 180.

Cram, G. 1901. "Panthers in Maine," *Forest & Stream.* 56(6): 123. Feb. 16.

Crane, J. 1931. "Mammals of Hampshire County, Massachusetts." *J. Mammal* 12(3): 267-273. August.

Cuvier, G. and E. Griffith. 1827. *The animal kingdom.* Vol. 2: 438-439. London.

Dashwood, R. L. 1871. *Chiploquorgan, or life by the camp fire in the Dominion of Canada and Newfoundland.* Robert T. White, 45 Fleet St., Dublin.

Dear, L. S. 1955. "Cougar or mountain lion reported in northwestern Ontario." *Can. Field-Nat.* 69(1).

Dearborn, N. 1927. "An old record of the mountain lion in New Hampshire." *J. Mammal.* 8(4): 311-312. Nov.

Dearborn, N. 1932. *Food of some predatory animals in Michigan.* School of Forestry and Cons. Bull. 1: 1-52, illus. Univ. Michigan. Ann Arbor. p. 50.

Dekay, J. E. 1842. "Zoology of New York and the New York fauna." Albany. I-XIII, 1-146. 33 pls.

Diereville, Sieur de. 1708. *Relation du voyage du Port Royal de L'Acadie, ou de la Nouvelle France.* Rouen.

Dietz, L. 1968. *The Allagash.* Rivers of America Series. Holt, Rinehart and Winston. New York, Chicago, San Francisco. 264 pp.

Dillin, J. G. 1924. *The Kentucky Rifle.* Nat. Rifle Ass'n of America. Washington, D.C. 124 pp.

Dionne, C. E. 1902. *Les mammifères de la province de Quebec.* Dussault & Proulx. Quebec. 285 pp., illus.

Doel, J. (Rev.). 1894. "The panther in Canada," *Biol. Rev. Ont.* 1(2): 18-23. April. Toronto.

Doutt, J. Kenneth. 1954. *Observations on mammals along the east coast of Hudson Bay and in the interior of Ungava.* Annals of the Carnegie Museum 33 Art 14. p. 243. Pittsburgh, Penn.

Doutt, J. K. 1968. "Mountain lions in Pennsylvania?" *Am. Soc. Mammal.* June 18, 1968.

169

↣ Doutt, J. K. 1969. "Mountain Lions in Pennsylvania?" *Am. Midland Natur-alist.* (82)1. July. 281-285.

Elliott, D. G. 1901. *A synopsis of the mammals of North America and the adjacent seas.* Field Columb. Mus. Zool. Series, Pub. 45. Vol. 11. 471 pp.

Elliott, D. G. 1904. "The land and sea mammals of Middle America and the West Indies." Field Columb. Mus. Zool. Series 4, part 2. 447-850.

Ely, A. and R. R. M. Carpenter. 1939. *North American big game.* Compiled by the Committee on Records of North American big game. Scribner's.

Emmons, E. 1840. *Report on the quadrupeds of Massachusetts.* Cambridge, Mass. 86 pp.

Evermann, B. W. and A. W. Butler. 1893. "Preliminary list of Indiana mammals." Proc. Ind. Acad. Sci: 120-139.

🐾 ✳ Faulkner, C. E. 1971. *The legal status of the wild cats in the United States.* Trans North American Wildlife and Natural Resources Conference. Portland, Oregon.

Faull, J. H. 1913. *The natural history of the Toronto region, Ontario, Canada.* Canad. Inst. Toronto. 419 pp.

Flint, T. 1856. *The first white-man of the west, or the life and exploits of Colonel Daniel Boone.* Cincinnati. 74 pp.

Foote, L. E. 1944. *A history of wild game in Vermont.* Vt. Fish & Game Service. State Bull. Pittman-Robertson Series 11: 46. Illus.

Funkhouser, W. D. 1925. *Wild life in Kentucky.* Ky. Geol. Surv. Frankfort. 385 pp.

"G. S. W." 1875. "Panthers in Vermont," *Forest & Stream* 5: 300.

Ganong, W. F. 1903. "On reported occurrences of the panther (*Felis concolor*) in New Brunswick." Bull. Nat. Hist. Soc. N.B., 21: 82-86.

Garman, H. 1894. *A preliminary list of the vertebrate animals of Kentucky.* Bull. Essex Inst. 26(1, 2, 3): 2-3. Jan., Feb., March. 63 pp.

Gesner, A. 1847. *New Brunswick* (including a catalogue of mammals). London. Simmonds and Ward.

Gilpin, J. B. 1864. "On the mammalia of Nova Scotia." Trns. N.S. Inst. Sci. 1(3): 8-15.

Gilpin, J. B. 1868. "On the mammalia of Nova Scotia." Trans. N.S. Inst. Sci. 2(2): 58-69.

Goertz, J. W. and R. Abegg. 1966. "Pumas in Louisiana," *J. Mammal.* 47(4): 727. Nov.

Goodwin, G. G. 1932. "New records and some observations of Connecticut mammals," *J. Mammal.* 13(1): 36-40.

Goodwin, G. G. 1935. *The mammals of Connecticut.* Bull. State Geol. and Nat. Hist. Surv. 53: 84-86. Hartford. 221 pp. illus.

Goodwin, G. G. 1936. "Big game animals of the northeastern United States," *J. Mammal.* 17(1): 48-50.

Gosse, P. H. 1840. *The Canadian naturalist.* John Van Noost, London. 372 pp.

Greenbie, S. 1929. *Frontiers and the Fur Trade.* New York. Feb. 208 pp.

Gregory, T. 1936. *Mammals of the Chicago region.* Chicago Acad. Sci. 7(2 & 3): 21. July, 74 pp. illus.

Gregory, T. 1938. "Lion in the Carmens," *The Chicago Naturalist.* Chi. Acad. Sci. 1(3): 70-81, 1(4): 110-120.

Hahn, W. L. 1909. "The mammals of Indiana." 33rd Annual Report, Indiana Dept. Geol. & Nat. Res. Indianapolis. Illus. 417-663.

170

Hall, A. 1861. "On the mammals and birds of the district of Montreal." Canad. Nat. & Geol. & Proc. Nat. Hist. Soc. Montreal, Canada. 6: 284-309.

Hall, E. R. and K. R. Kelson. 1959. *The Mammals of North America.* Ronald Press, New York. Vol. II.

Hallock, C. 1877. *The sportsman's gazetteer and general guide.* New York. 209 pp.

Hallock, C. 1880. *The sportsman's gazetteer and general guide.* Forest & Stream Pub. Co. N.Y. Ed. 5, part I, 700 pp. Part II 208 pp.

Hamilton, J. W. 1939. *American Mammals.* McGraw-Hill, New York.

Hamilton, J. W. 1943. *The mammals of the eastern United States.* Comstock, N.Y.

Handley, C. O. Jr., R. Stafford and E. H. Geil. 1961. "A West Virginia puma," *J Mammal.* 42(2): 277-278.

Hariot, T. 1587. *A brief and true report of the new found land of Virginia:* 33 pp.

Harlan, R. 1825. "Fauna Americana; being a description of the mammiferous animals inhabiting North America." Phila.: 94-95.

Harper, F. 1920. "Okefenokee Swamp as a reservation," *Nat. Hist.* 20: 29-40; 29. Jan. Feb.

Harper, F. 1926. "Tales of the Okefenokee," *American Speech.* 1: 408-420. May.

Harper, F. 1927. "The mammals of the Okefenokee Swamp region of Georgia." Proc. Bost. Soc. Nat. Hist. 37(7): 191-396.

Harper, F. 1945. "Extinct and vanishing mammals of the Old World." Am. Comm. Intern. Wildlife Prot. Special Bull. 12. N.Y. Zoological Park.

Henderson, A. 1920. *The conquest of the old southwest: the romantic story of the early pioneers into Virginia, the Carolinas, Tennessee, and Kentucky 1740-1790.* 395 pp.

Hewitt, C. G. 1921. *The Conservation of Wild Life in Canada.* New York. 344 pp.

Hibbard, C. W. 1943. "A check-list of Kansas mammals." Trans. Kans. Acad. Sci. 47: 61-88.

Hibben, F. C. 1937. *A preliminary study of the mountain lion.* Univ. New Mexico Bull. Biol. Series (5)3. Dec. 15th.

Hitchcock, C. H. 1862. *Catalogue of the mammals of Maine.* Proc. Portland Soc. Nat. Hist. 1: 65.

Hollingsworth, S. 1787. *The present state of Nova Scotia.* 2nd Ed. William Creach. Edinburgh.

Hollister, N. 1908. "Notes on Wisconsin mammals." Bull. Wisc. Nat. Hist. Soc. 4 (3-4): 1 & 1. Oct.

Hornocker, M. G. 1967. "An analysis of mountain lion predation upon mule deer and elk in the Idaho Primitive Area." PhD Thesis. Univ. British Columbia.

Hornocker, M. G. 1969. "Winter territoriality in mountain lions," *J. Wildl. Mgmt.* (33) 3: 457-464.

Imlay, G. 1793. *A topographical description of the western territory of North America.* London. 2nd Ed. 459 pp.

Ingersoll, E. 1906. *The life of animals. The mammals.* New York. 555 pp.

Jackson, C. F. 1922. "Notes on New Hampshire mammals," *J. Mammal.* 3(1): 13-15.

171

Jackson, H. H. T. 1908. *A preliminary list of Wisconsin mammals.* Bull. Wisc. Nat. Hist. Soc. 6(1-2): 14.

Jackson, H. H. T. 1943. "Conserving endangered wildlife species." Trans. Wisc. Acad. Sci. Arts & Letters. 35: 61-90.

Jackson, H. H. T. 1961. *Mammals of Wisconsin.* Univ. Wisc. Press. Madison. 511 pp.

Jardine, Sir Wm. 1934. *Naturalists' library.* Vol. 2. Mammals. Felidae: 266.

Jenkins, J. H. 1953. *The game resources of Georgia.* Ga. Game & Fish Comm. 98 pp.

Jenkins, J. H. 1971. "The status and management of the bobcat and cougar in the southeastern States." Trans. 36th N.A. Wildl. and Nat. Resources Conference. Portland, Ore.

Johnson, M. L. and L. H. Couch. 1954. "Determination of the abundance of cougar," *J. Mammal.* 35(2): 255-256.

Jones, G. W. 1945. "Virginia was once England's wild west," *Nature Mag.* 38(6): 317-320.

Keaton, J. B. 1940. "Bolivar my cougar chum," *Outdoor Life.* December.

Keller, W. P. 1966. *Under wilderness skies.* McLelland and Stewart, Toronto. 304 pp. illus.

Kellogg, R. 1937. "Annotated list of West Virginia mammals." Proc. U.S. Nat. Mus. 84(3022): 443-479.

Kellogg, R. 1939. "Annotated list of Tennessee mammals." Proc. U.S. Nat. Mus. Smiths. Inst. 86(3051): 245-303.

Kennicott, R. 1855. "Catalogue of animals observed in Cook County, Illinois." Trans. Ill. Agric. Soc. 1: 578-595. Springfield.

Kerr, R. 1792. *The animal kingdom.* 644 pp.

King, Major W. R. 1866. *The sportsman and naturalist in Canada.* Hurst & Blacket. London. 234 pp.

Kirtland, J. P. 1838. "A catalogue of the mammalia birds, reptiles, fishes, testacea and crustacea in Ohio." 2nd Ann. Report. Geol. Surv. Ohio. 160-200.

Lambert, H. 1955. "There ain't no 'painters' in West Virginia," *W. Va. Cons.* 19(1): 10-12. Illus. Mar.

Lane, F. N. 1939. *Nature parade.* Jarrolds. London.

Lapham, I. A. 1853. "Systematic catalogue of the mammals of Wisconsin." Trans. Wisc. Agric. Soc. 2: 337-340.

Larson, J. S. 1963. "Panthers in Maryland?" *The Maryland Cons.* Vol. XLIII (4).

Lawson, J. 1718. *The history of North Carolina.* T. Warner, London. 258 pp.

Lett, W. P. 1887. "The cougar or panther," *Ottawa Nat.* 1(9): 127-132. Dec.

Linsley, J. H. (Rev.). 1824. "Catalogue of the mammals of Connecticut," *Am. Jour. Sci. & Arts.* 43: 348. New Haven.

Lucas, J. 1948. "The mountain lion," *Sports Afield.* Dec.

Lueth, F. X. 1944. "Those we've had," *Ill. Cons.* 9(1): 14-15. Springfield.

Lyon, M. W. 1936. "Mammals of Indiana," *Am. Midl. Nat.* 17(1): 1-384.

Maclure, J. O. 1947. "Letter to the editor," *Field & Stream.* December.

Maine, State of. 1861. *Sixth annual report of Secretary, Maine Board of Agric.* 123. Augusta.

Manville, R. 1951. "Reports of cougar in New York," *J. Mammal.* 32(2): 227.

Marge, W. B. 1945. "Some extinct wild animals of Tidewater," *Md. Tidewater News* 2(1): 1,3. June. Solomons. Md.

Maxwell, H. 1898. *The history of Randolph County, West Virginia.* Morgantown. 531 pp. Illus.

McQueen, A. S. and H. Mizell. 1926. *History of Okefenokee Swamp.* Clinton, S.C. 191 pp.

McWhorter, L. V. 1915. *The border settlers of northwestern Virginia, from 1768 to 1795, embracing the life of James Hughes and other noted scouts of the great woods of the Trans-Allegheny, with notes and illustrative anecdotes.* Hamilton, Ohio. 509 pp.

Mearns, E. A. 1898. "Notes on the mammals of the Catskill Mountains, New York, with general remarks on the fauna and flora of the region." Smithson. Inst. Nat. Mus. Proc. 21(1147): 341-360.    (

Mearns, E. A. 1900. "The native mammals of Rhode Island." Circular, Newport Nat. Hist. Soc. 1: 1-4; July 1. Newport.

Merriam, C. H. 1882. "The vertebrates of the Adirondack region, northeastern New York." Trans. Linn. Soc. New York 1: 29-30.

Merriam, C. H. 1884. "The mammals of the Adirondack region." Foster, New York. 29-39.

Merriam, C. H. 1888. "Remarks on the fauna of the Great Smoky Mountains," *Am. Jour. Sci.* Series 3, Vol. 36 (216): 458-460.

Merriam, C. H. 1901. "Preliminary revision of the pumas *(Felis concolor* group)." Proc. Wash. Acad. Sci. 3: 577-600. Dec. 11.

Miller, G. S. Jr. 1899. "Preliminary list of New York mammals." Bull. N.Y. State Mus. 6(29): 270-390. Univ. New York.

Miller, G. S. Jr. and R. Kellogg. 1955. *List of North American recent mammals.* U.S. Nat. Mus. Bull. #205. Smiths. Inst. Washington, D.C. 954 pp.

Mills, W. C. 1907-1920. *Certain mounds and village sites in Ohio.* Columbus, Ohio. 4 vols.

Milne, J. W. 1894. "The panther in Canada," *Biol. Rev. Ont.* 1(4): 81-83. Toronto, Oct.

Monroe, A. 1855. *New Brunswick, Nova Scotia and P.E.I.* Nugent, Halifax. 384. pp.

Moorehead, W. K. 1922. *A report on the archaeology of Maine.* Andover Press, Andover, Mass. 272 pp.

Morris, R. F. 1948. "The land mammals of New Brunswick," *J. Mammal.* 29(2): 165-176.

Mountfort, Guy. 1970. "The Bengal tiger enters the Red Book." *Animals* July. 110-112.

Nash, C. W. 1908. *Manual of vertebrates of Ontario.* Dept. of Education, Toronto. Sect. 4: 96.

Nelson, E. W. 1916. "The larger North American mammals," *Nat. Geo. Soc.* (Nov.): 385-472. Washington, D.C.

Nelson, E. W. 1918. *Wild Animals of North America.* Nat. Geo. Soc. Washington, D.C. 254 pp.

Nelson, E. W. and E. A. Goldman. 1929. "List of the pumas, with three described as new," *J. Mammal.* 10(4): 345-350.

Newhouse, S. 1869. *The trappers guide.* Ed. 3, by Oneida Community, New York. Oakley, Mcoon & Co. New York.

Norton, A. H. 1930. "Mammals of Portland, Maine, and vicinity." Proc. Portland Soc. Nat. Hist. 4(Part 1): 49-51.

Oberholser, H. C. 1905. "Notes on the mammals and summer birds of western North Carolina." Biltmore Forestry School. Biltmore, N.C. 1-24. Sept. 30.

Orr, J. E. 1908. "The last panther," *Rod & Gun* and *Motor Sports in Canada.* 10(3): 266. August.

Orr, J. E. 1909. 1. "Some odd reminiscences of Old Ontario," *Rod & Gun* and *Motor Sports in Canada.* 10(9): 840-842.

Orr, J. E. 1909. 2. "Old time Stories of Ontario, *Rod & Gun* and *Motor Sports in Canada.* 11(3): 259-261. Aug.

Orr, J. E. 1911. "Old Time Stories of Old Ontario," *Rod & Gun* and *Motor Sports in Canada.* 12(11): 1439-1446. April.

Osgood, F. L. 1938. "The mammals of Vermont," *J. Mammal.* 19(4): 435-441. Nov.

Parsons, P. A. 1953. "All over the map," *Outdoor Life.* July.

"Peregrinus". 1824. "A panther hunt in Pennsylvania," *Port Folio.* Phila.: 31 (266): 494-499. June.

Peterson, R. L. 1966. *The mammals of eastern Canada.* Toronto. Oxford Press.

Philp. J. 1861. *Philp's Washington described.* Ed. by Wm. D. Haley, New York. Rudd & Carleton, Publ. 239 pp.

Pierce, J. 1823. *A memoir on the Catskill Mountains, with notices of their topography, scenery, minerology, zoology and economic resources.* Amer. J. Sci. & Arts. 6: 93.

Pocock, R. I. 1917. "The classification of existing Felidae," *Ann. Mag. Nat. Hist.* Ser. 8, Vol. 20: 329-350. Nov.

Porter, J. H. 1903. *Wild beasts.* Chas. Scribner's Sons. New York. 380 pp.

Powell, S. A. (Rev.) 1885. "Vermont deer and panther," *Forest & Stream* 25: 306.

Preble, E. A. 1908. "A biological investigation of the Athabasca-MacKenzie Region," *N.A. Fauna* 27: 208-209. Bur. Biol. Surv. U.S.D.A. Washington, D.C.

Rafinesque, C. S. 1832. "On the North American cougars," *Atlantic Journal and Friend of Knowledge.* 1(2): 51-56.

Ramsey, J. G. M. 1853. *The annuals of Tennessee to the end of the 18th century.* Phila. 749 pp.

Reilly, E. M. Jr. 1964. "New York's spooky big cats," *The Conservationist.* 18(4): 2-4.

Rhoads, S. N. 1896. "Contributions to the zoology of Tennessee." Proc. Acad. Nat. Sci. Phila. 48: 175-205.

Rhoads, S. N. 1903. *Mammals of Pennsylvania and New Jersey.* 266 pp.

Roberts, Sir C. G. D. 1896. *Around the camp-fire.* Thos. W. Crowell and Co. Boston.

Roberts, Sir C. G. D. 1902. *The watchers of the camp-fire.* The Page Co. Boston. 49 pp. Illus.

Robinette, W. L., J. S. Gashwiler and O. W. Morris. 1959. "Food habits of the cougar in Utah and Nevada." *J. Wildl. Mgmt.* 23(3): 261-273.

Robinette et al. 1961. "Notes on cougar productivity and life history," *J. Mammal.* 42(2): 204-217.

Samuels, E. A. 1863. "Mammalogy and ornithology in New England." Report, Comm. Agric.: 265-286. Govt. Printing Office, Washington, D.C.

Sass, H. R. 1954. "The panther prowls the east again," *Sat. Evening Post.* 226 (37): 31.

Schoepf, D. J. 1911. *Travels in the confederation, 1783-1784.* Phila.: 107-108.

Schorger, A. W. 1938. "A Wisconsin specimen of the cougar," *J. Mammal.* 19(2): 252. May.

174

Schorger, A. W. 1942. "Extinct and endangered mammals and birds of the upper Great Lakes region." Trans. Wisc. Acad. Sci., Arts & Letters. 34: 23-44.

Schwartz, C. W. and E. R. 1959. *The wild animals of Missouri*. Univ. of Missouri Press.

Scott, J. A. 1807. *A geographical description of the states of Maryland and Delaware*.

Scott, W. B. 1929. *A history of land mammals in the Western Hemisphere*. MacMillan Co. New York.

Scott, W. E. 1939. "Rare and extinct mammals of Wisconsin." Wisc. Cons. Bull. 4(10): 21-28. Oct.

Seagears, C. 1955. "Feline flying saucer," *The New York State Conservationist*, Dec.

Seton, E. T. 1918. In E. W. Nelson *Wild animals of North America*. Nat. Geo. Soc. Washington, D.C.

Seton, E. T. 1929. *Lives of Game Animals* Vol. I. *Cats, wolves and foxes*. Doubleday, Doran and Co. Garden City. Brantford reprint. Boston. 1953.

Shields, G. O. 1890. *The big game of North America*. Rand McNally & Co. Chicago and New York. 581 pp., illus.

Shoemaker, Col. H. W. 1913. "Stories of Pennsylvania animals," *Altoona Tribune*. 9-13.

Shoemaker, Col. H. W. 1914. *The Pennsylvania lion or panther*. The Altoona Tribune Co., Altoona, Pa. 23: 20.

Shoemaker, Col. H. W. 1917. *Extinct Pennsylvania animals*. Altoona Tribune Pub. Co. Altoona, Pa. 134 pp.

Shoemaker, Col. H. W. 1943. "The panther in Pennsylvania." Penna. Game Comm. Harrisburg. 13(11). Feb.

Silver, Helenette. 1957. *A history of New Hampshire game and furbearers*. Survey Report #6. N.H. Fish & Game Dept. Concord, N.H. May. 466 pp.

Smith, E. R., J. B. Funderburg and T. L. Quay. 1960. *A checklist of North Carolina mammals*. N.C. Wildlife Res. Comm. 19 pp.

Smith, Capt. J. 1884. *Captain John Smith's works* (1608-1631). Ed. by E. Arber Birmingham. 1199 pp.

Smith, R. W. 1940. "The land mammals of Nova Scotia," *Amer. Mid. Nat.* 24(1): 213-241.

Smith, S. 1765. *The history of the colony of Nova-Caesaria or New Jersey*. James Parker, Burlington, N.J., David Hall, Phila. 573 pp.

Smucker, I. 1876. *Centennial history of Licking County, Ohio*. Clark & Underwood. Newark, O. 80 pp.

Spargo, J. 1950. *The catamount in Vermont*. Bennington, Vt.

Springer, John. 1851. *Forest Life and Forest Trees*. Harper & Bros. New York.

Squires, W. A. 1946. "Changes in mammal populations in New Brunswick." *Acadian Nat.* 2: 26-44.

Squires, W. A. 1950. "The eastern panther is not extinct." *Can. Geo. Journ.* XLI (4). Oct.

Stone, W. 1908. "The mammals of New Jersey." Ann. Rept. N.J. State Mus. (1907). Trenton. 33-110.

Stone, W. and Wm. Cram. 1902. *American mammals*. 318 pp.

Stoner, D. 1950. *Extant New York specimens of the Adirondack cougar*. Circ. 25. N.Y. State Mus. Albany. May.

175

Thomas, W. 1896. *Great cats I have met; adventures in two hemispheres.* Alpha Pub. Co. Boston. 179 pp.

Thompson, Z. 1853. *The natural history of Vermont.*

Thoreau, H. D. 1858. "Chesuncook," *Atlantic Monthly.* June, July, August. Boston.

Thornton, J. F. 1956. "Mountain lion comeback in Alabama," *Alabama Cons.* March-April.

Tinsley, J. B.1970. *The Florida Panther.* Great Outdoors Publishing Company. St. Petersburg, Fla. 60 pp.

Trautman, M. B. 1939. "The numerical status of some mammals throughout historic time in the vicinity of Buckeye Lake, Ohio." Ohio Journ. Sci. 39(3): 136. May.

Trethewey, D. E. 1970. "The cougar in New Brunswick." Fish and Wildlife Newsletter. (2)3. July. Dept. of Natural Resources, Fredericton, 8-11.

True, F. W. 1889. "The puma or American lion. *Felis concolor* of Linnaeus." Rept. U.S. Nat. Mus. 591-608.

Tyrrell, J. B. 1888. *The mammalia of Canada.* Read before the Canadian Inst. April 7, and publ. in advance. Toronto.

Van Der Donck, A. 1656. *A description of the New Netherlands.* Coll. N.Y. Hist. Soc. Ed Z. (1): 167.

Walker, E. P. 1964. *Mammals of the world.* Vol. II. Johns Hopkins. Baltimore.

Walsh, W. 1956. "Panthers are popular," *Pa. Game News.* 27(1): 4-10. Jan.

Warden, D. B. 1819. *Statistical, political and historical account of the United States of North America. From the period of their first colonization to the present day.* 3 vols. Edinburgh.

White, G. 1849. *Statistics of Georgia.* W. Thorne Williams. Savannah, Ga. 624 pp.

Wildman, E. E. 1933. *Penn's woods, 1682-1932.* 192 pp.

Williams, S. C. 1930. *Beginnings of west Tennessee. In the land of the Chicksaws, 1541-1841.* Watange Press. Johnson City. 338 pp.

Wood. N. A. 1914. *An annotated checklist of Michigan mammals.* Occas. Papers Mus. Zool. Univ. Mich. 4:8 Ann Arbor.

Wood, N. A. 1922. "The mammals of Washtenaw County, Michigan." Occas. Papers, Mus. Zool. Univ. Mich. 123: 1-23. July 10.

Wright, B. S. 1948. 1. "Survival of the northeastern panther (*Felis concolor*) in New Brunswick, " *J. Mammal.* 29(3): 235-246.

Wright, B. S. 1948. 2. "The Fundy lions," *Field & Stream.* September. 54: 118-119.

Wright, B. S. 1953. "Further notes on the panther in the northeast," *Can. Field-Nat.* 67(1): 12-28.

Wright, B. S. 1954. "Don't shoot to prove there is one," *Hunting and Fishing in Canada.* Nov.

Wright, B. S. 1959. *The ghost of North America.* Vantage Press. New York. 140 pp. illus.

Wright, B. S. 1960. "Return of the cougar," *Audubon Mag.* Nov.-Dec. 262-265, 292-296. Illus., 1 map.

Wright, B. S. 1961. "The latest specimen of the eastern puma," *J. Mammal.* 42(2): 278-279.

Wright, B. S. 1964. "The wild cats of North America," *Animals.* March 3, 1964: 357-363.

176

Wright, B. S. 1965. 1. "Rediscovering the eastern panther," *Animals.* 6(4): 85. March.

Wright, B. S. 1965. 2. "The cougar in eastern Canada." *Can. Audubon* 27(5): 144-148.

York, William. 1971. "Notes on a study of serval melanism in the Aberdares and some general behavioral information." International Symposium on the Ecology, Behavior and Conservation of the World's Cats. Lion Country Safari, California.

Young, S. P. 1943. "Early wildlife Americana." *American Forests.* 49(8): 387-389, 414.

Young, S. P. 1946. *Sketches of American Wildlife.* The Monumental Press, Baltimore, Maryland.

Young, S. P. 1954. "The return of the 'Indian Devil'," *Pa. Game News.* 25(12)· 8-14. Illus. Dec.

Young, S. P. and E. A. Goldman. 1940 *The puma: mysterious American cat.* Am. Wildlife Institute. Washington, D.C. 358 pp.

Zeigler, W. G. 1883. *The heart of the Alleghenies; or western North Carolina.* 386 pp.

# INDEX

Acadia Forest Experiment Station, N.B., 49

Adams, Surgeon-Major A. Leith, 23

Aldergrounds, N.B., 54

Allen, H.B., 157

Anderson, Alfred, 97, 164

Anderson, Dr. R.M., Ack.

Anderson, Thomas, 95, 163

Antigonish, N.S. Fish & Game Association, 86, 162

Argue, Dr. C.W., Ack.

Badger, B.M., 165

Banks, D.B., 161

Barette, Dr. J.M., 40

Base Gagetown, N.B., 32, 40

Baxter, Minister of Justice J.B.M. and Mrs., 78, 161

Beadle Brook, N.B., 52

Becaguimec Game Refuge, N.B., 36, 47

Beck, Joe, 17, 155

Belyea, Herman, 74, 161

Benson, Denis, Ack.

Birdton School, N.B., 43, 44, 140

Bishop, Mrs. Otho H., 71, 160

Boardman, G.A., 12, 13, 79

Bondurant, Lt., 157

Bovey, Martin, 89, 162

Boyd, Cpl. W.F., 34, 156

Brown, Claxton, 103, 164

Butterwick, Dr. D.B., 40, 157

Caanan Game Refuge, 68

calls of a panther, 124-6

Careef, Hazen, 159

Catamount Station, N.B., 68

Chapman, Frank M., 136-7

Cherokee Indians, 7

Chesley, Dr. Arthur S., 67, 159

Chickasaw Indians, 7

Chute, Gerald, 40, 157

Clarke, Dr. C.H.D., Ack., 96

Clarke, Dr. George Frederic, 38

Claudie Road, 46

Claudie Settlement, 45

Cleghorn, D.J., 94

Cleghorn, Mrs. Ruth, 31, 156

Cody, Norman, 142

Cody, Mrs. Thelma, 48-9, 158

Collett, Victor, 31, 156

colours of a panther, 122-4

Colpitts, Pearl and Connie, 161

Cooney, R., 12

Corey, Game Warden David, 37

Corey, Sue, 21, 155

Crawford, Mrs. John, 142

Creek Indians, 7

Crossette, George, 164

Currie, Donald G., 39, 42, 157

Cyr, Raymond, 160

Dale, Bonneycastle, 69

De Lucry, William, 157

De Mond, L.R., 155

Devaney, Lt. R.H.C., 35-6, 157

Devon, N.B., 47

Diereville, Sieur de, 11

Dietz, Lew, 100

Dionne, C. E., 91

Dixon, Arthur C., 162

Dodds, Dr. Donald, Ack.

Donaldson, Harry N., 105, 164

Dorman, Lewis, 137

Doutt, J. Kenneth, 109

Dowker's Island, P.Q., 93

Driscoll, Mrs. Harry, 156

Dunbar, Dr. Max, 94

Duncanson, Lloyd, Ack., 83, 162

Duplessis, Bruce, 41, 157

Dykeman, Clairmont, 70, 160

East Thorndike, Maine, 98

Edmond, J.W., 114

Ellis, Dr. V.A., 141

Errington, Paul L., 146

Fairley, J.W., 65, 159

Farrell, Fred J., 97, 159, 164

*Field & Stream*, 3

Fox, Ashford, Ack.

Fraser, Collingwood, 66, 159

Fundy National Park, 1, 75

Fundy Trail, N.B., 1

Gabrielson, Dr. Ira N., Ack.

Gallant, John, 109, 165

Gamelin, Jacques, 90, 163

Ganong, W.F., 12-13, 78

Garner, Dr. William V., 105-6, 164

Gaudette, Conservation Officer Roland D., 104, 164

Geldart, Ernest T., 76, 161

Gesner, A., 12

Good, Burtt, 38

Gooseberry Cove Road, N.B., 16

Gorman, Hazen T., 27, 156

Gormley, Mr. S., 159

Grant, Fred, 55-6, 158

Grant, Roy, 69

Gray, Dick, 141

Green, Game Warden Harold W., 99, 164

Gregory, Tappan, 136

Grève, E., 90, 162

Gullison, John, 36, 157

Haig-Brown, Roderick, 125
Hallman, Noah, 137
Hammer, Senator Lucy, 106
Hanson, Guy H., 157
Hare, A.D., 111, 165
Hare, Cpl. Blair, 35, 157
Harlow, Walter, 101
Hattie, Albert, 86
Hemphill, Fred, 158
Hemphill, J.E., 160
Hodgson, Harry, 164
Hornocker, Dr. Maurice, 115-16, 121
Hubley, Sam, 143
Hudgman, Mr. and Mrs. Horace, 101
Hudson's Bay Company, 97, 95
Hungry Brook, N.B., 46
Hunter, Izaak, 93, 163

International Union for the Conservation of Nature and Natural Resources, Switzerland, 154

Jackson, Dr. H.H.T., 84
Johnson, Mrs. R.J., 71, 160
Jonas Bros., 92
*Journal of Mammalogy*, 3
Juniper, N.B., 53-4

Keaton, J.B., 126
Kennebecasis Valley, N.B., 70
Kinloch Plantation, 110
Kinney, M.I., 28, 156
Klandaghi, Lord of the Forest, 110

Lac des Quinze, P.Q., 95
Ladd, Game Warden Virgil E., 99, 164
Lawrence Station, N.B., 20
Lemming, John, 163
Leopold, Professor Aldo, Ack., 3, 145
Learo, The House of, 91, 163
Letourneau, Gene, Ack.
Levesque's Bog, N.B., 57
Lewis, Dr. Harrison F., Ack.
Lhoks, the, 8, 11, 12
Likely, Dr. J.C., 143, 155
Little Loon Lake, Guysborough Co., N.S., 85
Little River, N.B., 38, 46
Little St. John Lake, 91
Long, Dr. William J., 64, 159
lunxus, the, 8, 12
Lycoming County Consolidated Sportsman's Association, Pa., 108
Lynch, R.C.M.P. Constable D.L., 28, 156

Macdonald, H.A., 85-6, 162
MacDonald, J.D., 19

Maugerville, N.B., 48
Malecite Indians, 8, 11
Marr, Arley, 40, 157
Martin Head Panther Range, N.B., 2
Martin Head Panther Road, 72
Matheson, Earl, 155
Maynard, Charles J., 114
McArthur, Sandy, 25, 156
McDonald, J.D., 155
McDonald, Guide M., 30, 156
McGivney, F.H., 23
McIntyre, Frank, 20, 140-1, 155
McKnight, Freeman, Ack.
Membertou, Grand Sagamore of the Indians, 11
Mendall, Howard L., Ack.
Michaud, Ephraim, 27, 156
Micmac Indians, 8, 11
Miles, R.S., 29
Miller, George, 75, 161
Minguy, Claude, 89, 162
Moorehead, Ludwig K., Ack.
Morin, Rosarie, 91, 163
Myles, R.S., 141-2

Nashwaaksis panther, 37, 139
Natural History Society of New Brunswick, 12
Neill, J.G., 159
Nepisiguit Lake, N.B., 59
Nichols, White, 99, 164
Nixon, Mr., 15, 155
Noble, C. Gordon, 22, 155
Normandin, Jacques, Ack., 92

O'Brien, Forest Service Inspector W.J., 155
O'Donnell, A.W., 41, 157
Oliver, Steven, 156
Operation Indian Devil, 35-6

Paget, Earl, 158
Paim, Dr. Uno, 32
Penniac Ridge, N.B., 45
Penobscot Indians, 8
Perley, Dudley F., 126
pi-twal, the long-tailed one, 8, 12
Point Wolf River, N.B., 73
Pokiok, N.B., 24
Porcupine Lake, N.B., 15
Port Arthur, Ont., 96
Porter Brook, N.B., 64-5
Portobello Stream, N.B., 39, 48
Plummer, Henry, Ack.
Pridham, Harry, 143
Prince, Harold H., 161
Pugh, Edward, 24, 155, 159
Purdy, Hugh, 19, 155
Purvis, Col. Tex, 125

rabies, 74
Ramsay Brook, N.B., 61
Raynes, Charles T., 155
Redpath Museum, McGill University, 93, 94
Reid, Mrs. D.F., 76, 78, 161
Rivière du Chute, N.B., 52
Robb, Professor of Natural History at the University of New Brunswick, 23
Roberts, Sir Charles G.D., 14, 89, 162
Robertson, Havelock, 69, 160
Robinson, Charles Larned, Ack., 100, 164
Rosenbaum, Fred J., 165
Royal Canadian Mounted Police, 21, 28, 157
Royal Highland Regiment of Canada, 35
Russelltown, P.Q., 90

Sanford, Cpl., 157
Sangster, Walter, 155, 156
Sass, Herbert Ravenel, Ack., 110, 165
Sault Ste. Marie, Ont., 96
Saxe, Charles M., 164
Scarratt, Dr. and Mrs., 21, 155
Sears, Dr. J.W., 158
Senneville, P.Q., 93
Shaw, Charles, 161
Shoemaker, Col. Henry W., 106
Silver, Mrs. Helenette, Ack.
size of a panther, 113-15
Snow, Sheldon, 75
South La Grange, Maine, 97
St. Martins, N.B., 1
St. Zacharie, P.Q., 91
Ste. Anne de Bellevue, P.Q., 93

Steeves, Rflm., 34
Swedburg, Jack, 164
Sweet, Raymond, 158

Taber, Wendell, 125
Thorne, Mr., 22
Tingley, Game Warden John, 70, 160
Torrie, Dr. A.F., 155
Trethewey, Donald, 158
Tufts, Robie W., Ack., 79
Tweedie, Gordon C., 53

Ward's Natural History Establishment, N.Y., 95
Watts, Justice of the Peace Herman L., 108
Waugh, Lt.-Col. Freeman, 34, 35, 156
Waugh Ridge, N.B., 52
Weatherbee, Judge Randolph, 98, 164
Webb, Winford, 17, 155
Weeks, Fred, 19, 20, 155
West Long Lake, N.B., 16
White, Shirley, 43, 157
Whooper of the Dungarvon, 66
Wilcox, Charles, 99, 164
Wildlife Management Institute, Ack.
Wright, B.S., 156, 158, 160

Vanderbeck, Forest Ranger Perley W., 65, 159
Veness, J.C., 159

York Mills, N.B., 25, 30
Young, Stanley P., Ack., 84

Zuñi Indians, 7